Over This Soil

Over This Soil

An Anthology of
World Farm Poems

Edited by Catherine Webster

Foreword by James Galvin

University of Iowa Press Ψ Iowa City

University of Iowa Press,
Iowa City 52242
Copyright © 1998 by the
University of Iowa Press
All rights reserved
Printed in the United States of America
Design by Richard Hendel
http://www.uiowa.edu/~uipress

Printed on acid-free paper

Library of Congress
Cataloging-in-Publication Data
Over this soil: an anthology of world farm poems /
   edited by Catherine Webster; foreword by
   James Galvin.
        p.   cm.
     ISBN 0-87745-616-X, ISBN 0-87745-617-8
     1. Farm life — Poetry.   2. Domestic animals —
Poetry.   I. Webster, Catherine.
   PN6110.F34084   1998
808.81'9355 — DC21   97-33444
98 99 00 01 02 C 5 4 3 2 1
98 99 00 01 02 P 5 4 3 2 1

This anthology of farm poems is inscribed to Dennis Schmitz.

Carpent tua poma nepotes — Let the grandchildren gather the apples.
  Virgil, Eclogue IX

I'd gone out of the cave. Looked at the scaled brightness
of the sea ten miles away; looked at unfamiliar plants.
During the war, a botanist in Pusan had told me,
a number of native species had become extinct. People
in the countryside boiled anything that grew to make a soup.
  Robert Hass, *Sun under Wood*

Contents

Foreword

JAMES GALVIN

From Nature's point of view, if Nature had a point of view (maybe Nature is nothing but points of view?), the opposable thumb wired to a clever and curious neural center has got to be the most catastrophic development in the history of evolution. For at least 10,000 years human presence on earth has been characterized in great measure by heedless rapacity and destruction, except when the human presence is of insufficient density to matter.

Other than Art, which we do for ourselves or our gods, it is often difficult to think of traditional human activities that have not proved destructive to the earth whose earth we are.

Can the opposable thumb and the brain in opposition be used to enable, enhance, and revere life on earth rather than to grasp, control, throw out of balance?

There are examples of beneficial human stewardship, and the voices in the poems of this anthology are affirming not only that we must change course but that we can change course according to what we are beginning to understand and rediscover. This anthology of world farm poems may be the least explicitly philosophical compilation I can think of, and implicitly the most philosophical, treating as it does the ancient conversation with landscape and the mystery of Nature we call Agriculture.

Technology of any kind, from flint knapping to strip mining, rocketeering, particle busting, is a conversation we sustain, whether we know it or not, with Nature. For example, the conversation of strip mining, or industry in general, historically might be likened to the conversation a rapist has with his or her victim, while Environmentalism is mostly listening for the subtleties and catastrophes that are Nature's fluencies, trying to learn that language and learn from it.

But of all the conversations we have and have had with Nature, Agriculture is arguably the most immediate, intimate, lively, and potentially loving one, since it is ancient, most necessary, and since the answers of our interlocutor are comparatively clear and direct — like the conversation of a long-married, long-loving couple.

Infinitely oversimplified, it could go like this:

"Shall I till the soil?"

"Yes, if gently, diligently. Not on steeps or drainages."

"Shall I irrigate?"

"Yes, if intelligently and to vital purpose."

"How about tractors?"

"I preferred the horses and the oxen."

"How about grazing?"

"Imitate the wild herds' motions."

"Shall I control the pests and weeds with chemicals?"

"I'll leave you. And I'll leave you poor."

Etc.

(I'm pretty sure you'll find more horses than tractors in these pages. World agriculture is not American agriculture, nor should it ever be. Even in America we have the prophetic admonitions of the Mennonites and Amish.)

Who speaks for the land, or more properly, who interprets the language of subtlety and catastrophe? Poets? Farmers? Poet-farmers? What do you lose, from an environmental point of view, when you lose a family farm or ranch? Besides losing a way of life, a culture opposed to the dominant First World values of expansion and greed, you lose species diversity, care, and the thread of the conversation concerning a particular place. Generally speaking, one finds more species diversity on a large, well-managed ranch than one finds in a national park. What you get in return is a housing development, a vacation spot, forty-acre ranchettes, or a corporate entity whose only allegiance (however they protest) is to a quarterly bottom line.

Read these poems. There is wisdom here. Wisdom says tread lightly. Feel gratitude. Revere the source. Listen to the ancient, loving conversation that, by implication, includes everything — life, death, growth, nourishment, manners, fear, frustration, love, morality, humility, wonder — the most deeply philosophical utterances, with, as I said, hardly any philosophy.

Acknowledgments

To my family, Sarah and Brian Campbell, Matthew Vernon Marconi, Alberta Lewallen, Mark and Edwina, and Mark-John and Morley Lewallen to acknowledge their love.

To Kim and Marc Wolterbeek, Muriel and Rand Zeller, Phil Hutcheon and Joan Bailey, and Linda and John Hussa for their abiding friendship.

To Mayor Gary Podesto, Stockton, California, Ralph Grossi, president of American Farmland Trust, Washington, D.C., and to Jorie Graham and Jim Galvin for their vision.

To the Capecchino Foundation, the C. A. Webster Foundation, the Bank of Stockton, and Vincent A. Gaudiani to acknowledge the financial support that enabled me to pay for the permissions.

To Dean Robert Benedetti, University of the Pacific; UOP English Department chairpersons John Smith and Robert Cox; David Hamilton, the *Iowa Review;* and Daniel Weissbort, Department of Comparative Literature, the University of Iowa, for their consistent support.

To Jan Weissmiller, Prairie Lights Bookstore, Iowa City; Bill Maxwell, Maxwell's Bookstore, Stockton; City Lights Bookstore, San Francisco; and Kinko's in Stockton, Iowa City, and Laramie for their excellent research and technical help.

To Carolyn Eads, copartner in the preparation of this manuscript, to whom I am deeply grateful for her help with the development of this book. And to Katharine Stall, thank you.

And, of course, to Dennis Schmitz, to whom this book is dedicated, and to whom I repeatedly turn for inspiration, many, many thanks.

I
My Mother's Pears

My Mother's Pears
STANLEY KUNITZ *United States*

Plump, green-gold, Worcester's pride,
    transported through autumn skies
        in a box marked Handle With Care

sleep eighteen Bartlett pears,
    hand-picked and polished and packed
        for deposit at my door,

each in its crinkled nest
    with a stub of stem attached
        and a single bright leaf like a flag.

A smaller than usual crop,
    but still enough to share with me,
        as always at harvest time.

Those strangers are my friends
    whose kindness blesses the house
        my mother built at the edge of town

beyond the last trolley-stop
    when the century was young, and she
        proposed, for her children's sake,

to marry again, not knowing how soon
    the windows would grow dark
        and the velvet drapes come down.

Rubble accumulates in the yard,
    workmen are hammering on the roof,
        I am standing knee-deep in dirt

with a shovel in my hand.
    Mother has wrapped a kerchief round her head,
        her glasses glint in the sun.

When my sisters appear on the scene,
    gangly and softly tittering,
        she waves them back into the house

to fetch us pails of water,
    and they skip out of our sight
        in their matching middy blouses.

I summon up all my strength
    to set the pear tree in the ground,
        unwinding its burlap shroud.

It is taller than I. "Make room
    for the roots!" my mother cries,
        "Dig the hole deeper."

Fruit

GABRIELA MISTRAL *Chile*

In the white pasture of the sun,
fruit spills like chunks of gold.

The gold comes from Brazilian lands,
from the willowy darkness of Brazil's serenade.
My child, they send a clustered afternoon slumber.
I allow the glorious abundance to roll:
colors wheel with fragrance.

Crawling, you pursue the fruits
as though they were little girls,
scattering in all directions:
melting loquats
and hard, tattooed pineapples . . .

And all the things exude the aroma of Brazil,
breast of the world which they suckled.
Although not enjoying Atlantic water,
nevertheless, they could overflow its skirt.

Touch them, kiss them, whirl them,
and learn their faces.
Dream, child, that your mother
has ripened features;
the night is a black basket
and that the Milky Way is an orchard.

Translated by Maria Giachetti

What If the World Stays Always Far Off

LINDA GREGG *United States*

What if the world is taken from me?
If there is no recognition? My words unheard?
Keats wanted to write great poetry
and I am in the orchard all day.

The work is too hard and no one here
will do it. So they bring Jamaicans.
The men sometimes sing on their ladders.
Named Henry and George. "Yes, Boss," they say.
The bus brought them late this morning.
They not wanting to work because of the cold.
They walk slowly through the wet grass.
"Today we are not happy," they say going by me.

The grass is wet one to three hours.
Then dry. Sometimes everything is warm
and I wish the man I know would come
in his car and make love to me.

We do not speak much. Because of the work.
And because I am the only woman.
They see no women. Two months here picking apples.
Six in Florida cutting cane.

At night my body is so tired I don't want
to make love. I want to be alone and to sleep.
It is very beautiful in the fields under
the apple trees all day. I saw two night hawks
white with black wave designs counter to the wings.
The boss saw two hundred of them fly over
this valley once. Going south.
What if I continue unnoticed.

Foxes red and grey. Woodchucks. A pretty rabbit
on the road in the rain, confused and afraid.
Running suddenly toward the lights.

An apple has all colors. Even blue.
Much purple and maroon. (If there would be
no recognition and the world remains far away?)
The leaves are a duller green than the grass.
I pick McIntosh, but there are forty kinds
on the land around. Three hundred acres
near the next town. This is autumn in Massachusetts.
Not my home. I heard of beauty in New England
and the people. Came looking for love.

Nobody talks to the Jamaicans. They are driven
to Safeway in the bus and brought back.
I saw one alone just standing by the woods.
"I send money to my mother if I feel like it,"
he said to impress me. About eighteen.
He will cut cane for the first time this year.
"I hear the bosses are mean," I said.
"We make more money," he said. "It is a longer time."

Are you lost if there is no recognition?
Is beauty home? Is fear or pain?
An old man who drives the truck and has a farm
of his own down the road said,
"I just help during the harvest.
I have everything except apples. Lots of squash."
It made me happy to know they still say harvest.

I am here with them for the harvest. Thirty-six.
A woman. Canning when there's time. It will be
very cold soon. Already there are dark rains.

The Pitchfork

SEAMUS HEANEY *Ireland*

Of all implements, the pitchfork was the one
That came near to an imagined perfection:
When he tightened his raised hand and aimed with it,
It felt like a javelin, accurate and light.

So whether he played the warrior or the athlete
Or worked in earnest in the chaff and sweat,
He loved its grain of tapering, dark-flecked ash
Grown satiny from its own natural polish.

Riveted steel, turned timber, burnish, grain,
Smoothness, straightness, roundness, length and sheen.
Sweat-cured, sharpened, balanced, tested, fitted.
The springiness, the clip and dart of it.

And then when he thought of probes that reached the farthest,
He would see the shaft of a pitchfork sailing past
Evenly, imperturbably through space,
Its prongs starlit and absolutely soundless —

But has learned at last to follow that simple lead
Past its own aim, out to an other side
Where perfection — or nearness to it — is imagined
Not in the aiming but the opening hand.

The Bull-Roarer

GERALD STERN *United States*

I

I only saw my father's face in butchery
once — it was a horror — there were ten men
surrounding a calf, their faces were red, my father's
eyes were shining; there might have been fewer than ten,
some were farmers, some were my father's friends
down from the city. I was nine, maybe eight;
I remember we slept a few hours and left
at four in the morning, there were two cars, or three,
I think it was West Virginia. I remember
the pasture, the calf was screaming, his two eyes
were white with terror, there was blood and slaver
mixed, he was spread-eagled, there was a rope
still hanging from his neck, they all had knives
or ice picks — is that possible? — they were beery,
drunk, the blood was pouring from the throat
but they were stabbing him, one of them bellowed
as if he were a bull, he was the god
of the hunters, dressed in overalls and boots,
the king of animals; they seemed to know —
some of them seemed to know — the tendons and bones,
they were already cutting and slicing, pulling
the skin off, or maybe that was later, I stood there
staring at them, my father with a knife;
we didn't even have a dog — my mother froze
whenever she saw one — we were living in Beechview,
we had the newest car on the street, it was
an ugly suburb, everything was decent,
there was a little woods, but it was locust,
it would be covered with houses, we didn't even have
a parrot, my father left at eight in the morning
and drove his car downtown, he always wore
a suit and tie, his shoes were polished, he spent
the day with customers, he ate his lunch

9

at a little booth, I often sat with him,
with him and his friends, I had to show off, I drew
their likenesses, I drew the tables and chairs,
it was the Depression, none of them had brass rings
hanging from their ears, they all wore socks,
and long-sleeved shirts, they ate and drank with passion.

II

My mother is eighty-seven, she remembers
the visit to the farm, there was her brother,
my uncle Simon, and there was his friend, MacBride,
Lou MacBride, he was the connection, he was
a friend of the farmer's, maybe a cousin. I asked her
about the killing — "that is the way those farmers
got their meat, they lived like that, they butchered
whatever they needed." I asked if she could remember
anything strange, was she nervous or frightened?
"There was the tail, they cut the tail off
and chased each other; it was like pinning the tail
to the donkey." Both of us laughed. I didn't have the heart
to mention my father's face, or mention the knife —
and, most of all, my pain. What did I want?
That he should stay forever locked inside
his gold-flecked suits? That he should get up in the dark
and put his shoes on with a silver knife?
That he should unbutton his shirts and stuff the cardboard
into a chute? That he should always tie
his tie with three full loops, his own true version
of the Windsor knot? And what did I want for myself?
Some childish thing, that no one would ever leave me?
That there would always be logic — and loyalty?
— I think that tail goes back to the Paleolithic.
I think our game has gory roots — some cave,
or field, they chased each other — or they were grimmer,
pinning that tail, some power was amassed,
as well as something ludicrous, always that,
the tail was different from the horns, or paws,

it was the seat of shame — and there was envy,
not just contempt, but envy — horns a man has,
and he has furry hands and he has a mane,
but never a tail. I remember dimly
a toy we had, a kind of flattened stone,
curved at the sides, with a long rope at one end
we whirled around to make a thundering noise.
This was a "bull-roarer"; we made thunder
and felt the power in our shoulders and legs.
I saw this toy in southern Italy;
I saw children throwing it over their heads
as if they were in central Australia
or ancient Europe somewhere, in a meadow,
forcing the gods to roar. They call it Uranic,
a heavenly force, sometimes almost a voice,
locked up in that whirling stone, dear father.

Tractor

TED HUGHES *Great Britain*

The tractor stands frozen — an agony
To think of. All night
Snow packed its open entrails. Now a head-pincering gale,
A spill of molten ice, smoking snow,
Pours into its steel.
At white heat of numbness it stands
In the aimed hosing of ground-level fieriness.

It defies flesh and won't start.
Hands are like wounds already
Inside armor gloves, and feet are unbelievable
As if the toenails were all just torn off.
I stare at it in hatred. Beyond it
The copse hisses — capitulates miserably
In the fleeing, failing light. Starlings,
A dirtier sleetier snow, blow smokily, unendingly, over
Towards plantations eastward.
All the time the tractor is sinking
Through the degrees, deepening
Into its hell of ice.

The starting lever
Cracks its action, like a snapping knuckle.
The battery is alive — but like a lamb
Trying to nudge its solid frozen mother —
While the seat claims my buttock-bones, bites
With the space-cold of earth, which it has joined
In one solid lump.
I squirt commercial sure-fire
Down the black throat — it just coughs.
It ridicules me — a trap of iron stupidity
I've stepped into. I drive the battery
As if I were hammering and hammering
The frozen arrangement to pieces with a hammer

And it jabbers laughing pain-crying mockingly
Into happy life.

And stands
Shuddering itself full of heat, seeming to enlarge slowly
Like a demon demonstrating
A more than usually complete materialization —
Suddenly it jerks from its solidarity
With the concrete, and lurches towards a stanchion
Bursting with superhuman well-being and abandon
Shouting Where? Where?

Worse iron is waiting. Power-lift kneels,
Levers awake imprisoned deadweight,
Shackle pins bedded in cast-iron cow shit.
The blind and vibrating condemned obedience
Of iron to the cruelty of iron,
Wheels screeched out of their night locks —

Fingers
Among the tormented
Tonnage and burning of iron

Eyes
Weeping in the wind of chloroform

And the tractor, streaming with sweat,
Raging and trembling and rejoicing.

De Profundis

GEORG TRAKL *Germany*

It is a stubble field, where a black rain is falling.
It is a brown tree, that stands alone.
It is a hissing wind, that encircles empty houses.
How melancholy the evening is.

Beyond the village,
The soft orphan garners the sparse ears of corn.
Her eyes graze, round and golden, in the twilight
And her womb awaits the heavenly bridegroom.

On the way home
The shepherd found the sweet body
Decayed in a bush of thorns.

I am a shadow far from darkening villages.
I drank the silence of God
Out of the stream in the trees.

Cold metal walks on my forehead.
Spiders search for my heart.
It is a light that goes out in my mouth.

At night, I found myself in a pasture,
Covered with rubbish and the dust of stars.
In a hazel thicket
Angels of crystal rang out once more.

Translated by James Wright

Swineherd

EILEAN NI CHUILLEANAIN *Ireland*

When all this is over, said the swineherd,
I mean to retire, where
Nobody will have heard about my special skills
And conversation is mainly about the weather.

I intend to learn how to make coffee, at least as well
As the Portuguese lay-sister in the kitchen
And polish the brass fenders every day.
I want to lie awake at night
Listening to cream crawling to the top of the jug
And the water lying soft in the cistern.

I want to see an orchard where the trees grow in straight lines
And the yellow fox finds shelter between the navy-blue trunks,
Where it gets dark early in summer
And the apple-blossom is allowed to wither on the bough.

The Lithuanian Well

JOHANNES BOBROWSKI *Germany*

My paths out of sand, the heavens
over the willow thicket.
Wooden bucket, travel up.
Drench me with earth.

Hours away, lark, your song,
by the head of the hawk.
If the sower hears you,
the reaper has forgotten you.

Glance to the plowed-up field,
the carts are coming, the wind's howl.
Ladler-maid, lean into the light.
Sing your mouth pale.

Translated by Juliette Victor-Rood

Someone Else's Sugarcane

JOÃO CABRAL DE MELO NETO *Brazil*

I

The one who walks and plants
the joints of sugarcane
in no way is the Sower
that has been sonnetized.

His gesture is less a gesture
of love than of commerce;
the way he throws the cane,
he does not plant: he throws away.

2

Weeding the land, they work
in unison, to the cadence of hoes,
rough and disinterested,
of those who do without understanding.

As men who do not understand
why only this is weed,
rank and to be cleared,
but this, sugarcane, not.

3

In the sugarcane cutter
what is seen is the anger
that brings down a forest
not the love of a harvest.

The fury, anger, ferocious
enmity of one who mutilates,
of one who, without care,
hacks a trail through the woods.

4

The folks from the funeral home
in charge of the deceased,
instead of dressing the remains
bind them in bundles of bones.

When the procession arrives
the crude undertaker chucks
the can in the tomb-press
to be pressed in the living grave.

Translated by Ricardo da Silveira Lobo Sternberg

A Leopard Lives in a Muu Tree

JONATHAN KARIARA *Kenya*

A leopard lives in a Muu tree
Watching my home
My lambs are born speckled
My wives tie their skirts tight
And turn away —
Fearing mottled offspring.
They bathe when the moon is high
Soft and fecund
Splash cold mountain stream water on their nipples
Drop their skin skirts and call obscenities.
I'm besieged
I shall have to cut down the Muu tree
I'm besieged
I walk about stiff
Stroking my loins.
A leopard lives outside my homestead
Watching my women
I have called him elder, the one-from-the-same-womb
He peers at me with slit eyes
His head held high
My sword has rusted in the scabbard.
My wives purse their lips
When owls call for mating
I'm besieged
They fetch cold mountain water
They crush the sugar cane
But refuse to touch my beer horn.
My fences are broken
My medicine bags torn
The hair on my loins is singed
The upright post at the gate has fallen
My women are frisky
The leopard arches over my homestead
Eats my lambs
Resuscitating himself.

Heavier

PIERRE REVERDY *France*

They waited for the man stretched out
across the road to wake up. The curve of the night
stopped at the thatched cottage which was still lit
up, at the edge of the meadow, in front of the forest
which was closing its gates. All the freshness inside.
The animals were there only to enliven the landscape
while all the rest walked.

    For everything was walking, except the animals,
the landscape and me, who with that statue,
more immobile than the other one, was up there,
on the pedestal of clouds.

Translated by John Ashbery

Wo/men

CHIQUI VICIOSO *Dominican Republic*

Wo/men draped in black
multicolor socks and strong arms
hair and moustaches, hairy legs
hormones and hairs . . . patchy with suffering.
Sad women, who never smile
lacking teeth, lacking dreams
women / earth, dirt farm and hoes
women / cabbage, tomatoes and wool
women / man, child and tenderness
iron women, rock women.

Translated by Daisy Cocco de Filippis

Aunt Julia

NORMAN MacCAIG *Scotland*

Aunt Julia spoke Gaelic
very loud and very fast.
I could not answer her —
I could not understand her.

She wore men's boots
when she wore any.
— I can see her strong foot,
stained with peat,
paddling the treadle of the spinning wheel
while her right hand drew yarn
marvellously out of the air.

Hers was the only house
where I lay at night
in the absolute darkness
of the box bed, listening to
crickets being friendly.

She was buckets
and water flouncing into them.
She was winds pouring wetly
round house-ends.
She was brown eggs, black skirts
and a keeper of threepennybits
in a teapot.

Aunt Julia spoke Gaelic
very loud and very fast.
By the time I had learned
a little, she lay
silenced in the absolute black
of a sandy grave
at Luskentyre.
But I hear her still, welcoming me

with a seagull's voice
across a hundred yards
of peatscapes and lazybeds
and getting angry, getting angry
with so many questions
unanswered.

Waterpot

GRACE NICHOLS *Great Britain*

The daily going out
and coming in
always being hurried
along
like like . . . cattle

In the evenings
returning from the fields
she tried hard to walk
like a woman

she tried very hard
pulling herself erect
with every three or four
steps
pulling herself together
holding herself like
royal cane

And the overseer
hurrying them along
in the quickening darkness

And the overseer sneering
them along in the quickening
darkness

sneered at the pathetic —
the pathetic display
of dignity

O but look
there's a waterpot growing
from her head

The Earthworm

HARRY EDMUND MARTINSON *Sweden*

Who really respects the earthworm,
the farmworker far under the grass in the soil.
He keeps the earth always changing.
He works entirely full of soil,
speechless with soil, and blind.

He is the underneath farmer, the underground one,
where the fields are getting on their harvest clothes.
Who really respects him,
this deep and calm earth-worker,
this deathless, gray, tiny farmer in the planet's soil.

Translated by Robert Bly

Probably the Farmer

LAURA JENSEN *United States*

Probably the farmer hid in the valley
and kept his eye on his dog and son.
The English were hardly so. I think
they stood like the fools that cannot stop
rattling their basins under the sun,
opening their lungs to the dark blue fire
of the dragon boat's tongue. Probably
the farmer could believe what he heard:

I am cold. Yes I am the running drill
of ignorance that becomes sand, the disappointment
under the cliff, the eternal white claws
that intend to be kept.

Probably the farmer closed his eyes
and saw that they stood like fools
rattling their basins under morning,
opening their lungs into its fire.

Probably the farmer
had looked at the seashore and traveled
at least a mile on it, off the cliff,
not touching abalone, or mint,
or the stark or water-drunken trees;
but invented pockets to think by,
turned deliberately and walked home.

By his vision he directed his household.
If anything knew its way home he kept it;
when the seamen came they were so expected
that they killed only all the chickens,
ate only all he had.
In this way
the farmer became a citizen.

Farmers

KATHLEEN PEIRCE *United States*

Never able to enter
green, they did
what they knew how,
turned everything
to rooms, every
field a low room
with four corners,
four green points
to start
and rest from being
in love with green.
In one green room
in a big square house
a farmhouse whitewashed
white,
because to paint
a farmhouse green
would be too much
a valentine
to the field.
Also, being human,
there was that need
of a returning place
when so much is denied.

The Broken Ground

WENDELL BERRY *United States*

The opening out and out,
body yielding body:
the breaking
through which the new
comes, perching
above its shadow
on the piling up
darkened broken old
husks of itself:
bud opening to flower
opening to fruit opening
to the sweet marrow
of the seed —
    taken
from what was, from
what could have been.
What is left
is what is.

Between Each Song

A. R. AMMONS *United States*

I once would have said my sister Vida but now
I can just say my sister because the other

sister is gone: you didn't know Mona, lovely
and marvelous Mona, so you can't feel the

flooded solar plexus that grips me now: but
you may know (I don't know if I hope you will

or hope you won't — tossups between having and
holding) but you may know someone of your own

I don't quite know the pang for as you do: I
know but don't believe Mona is gone: she is

still so much with me, I can hardly tell I lost
anything when I lost so much: love is a very

strange winding about when it gets lost in
your body and especially when it can't find

the place to go to, the place it used to find: Mona is
in my heart in a way that burns my chest until

my eyes water: are you that way: even in the
midst of business I could think of caring for

you for that: but my sister Vida and I used
to have to daub (we called it dob) the baccer

barn: cracks between the uneven-log sides
had to be filled airtight with clay so the

furnace and flues could "cure" the tobacco
with slow, then high heat: we would dig a

bucket of clay from the ditch by the road
where streaks of white and red clay ran, add

water for a thick consistency, then climb the
rafters inside the barn and dob the cracks:

can you imagine: kids: (perhaps it beat
empty streets filled with drugs): I REALLY
THINK WE SHOULD GET IT OFF OR GET OFF IT

Hunger

KIM CHI HA *Korea*

Ah, my belly's empty!
Pulling up weeds
I lie down and drink spring water,
Use a rock as my pillow.
I'll eat roots, gulp down dirt and wild flowers,
Bright red poison mushrooms,
Yet still have an empty belly.
I could devour animals by the hundreds, thousands — hard ones.
I want to eat pork, put away fat ones.
I'll eat you.
I've been driven mad by long starvation,
Dragging this enormous empty gut along the ground.
I will leave the country where there is nothing to eat
And go to Seoul,
Picking up food along the way:
Fishbones, sprouts,
Rib-bones leftover by the dogs,
Eggs, houses, streets,
Pieces of iron.
Male and female,
Anything that has grown fat —
I'll even eat human flesh.
Ah, I'm so unbearably hungry
I could eat money.

II

The United Fruit Co.

The Right Hand of a Mexican Farmworker in Somerset County, Maryland

MARTÍN ESPADA *United States*

A rosary tattoo
between thumb
and forefinger
means that
every handful
of crops and dirt
is a prayer,
means that Christ
had hard hands
too

The Onion

WISLAWA SZYMBORSKA *Poland*

The onion, now that's something else.
Its innards don't exist.
Nothing but pure onionhood
fills this devout onionist.
Oniony on the inside,
onionesque it appears.
It follows its own daimonion
without our human tears.

Our skin is just a coverup
for the land where none dare go,
an internal inferno,
the anathema of anatomy.
In an onion there's only onion
from its top to its toe,
onionymous monomania,
unanimous omninudity.

At peace, of a piece,
internally at rest.
Inside it, there's a smaller one
of undiminished worth.
The second holds a third one,
the third contains a fourth.
A centripetal fugue.
Polyphony compressed.

Nature's rotundest tummy,
its greatest success story,
the onion drapes itself in its
own aureoles of glory.
We hold veins, nerves, and fat,
secretions' secret sections.
Not for us such idiotic
onionoid perfections.

Translated by Stanislaw Baranczak and Clare Cavanagh

The United Fruit Co.
PABLO NERUDA *Chile*

When the trumpets had sounded and all
was in readiness on the face of the earth,
Jehovah divided his universe:
Anaconda, Ford Motors,
Coca-Cola Inc., and similar entities:
the most succulent item of all,
The United Fruit Company Incorporated
reserved for itself: the heartland
and coasts of my country,
the delectable waist of America.
They rechristened their properties:
the "Banana Republics"—
and over the languishing dead,
the uneasy repose of the heroes
who harried that greatness,
their flags and their freedoms,
they established an *opéra bouffe*:
they ravished all enterprise,
awarded the laurels like Caesars,
unleashed all the covetous, and contrived
the tyrannical Reign of the Flies—
Trujillo the fly, and Tacho the fly,
the flies called Carias, Martinez,
Ubico—all of them flies, flies
dank with the blood of their marmalade
vassalage, flies buzzing drunkenly
on the populous middens:
the fly-circus fly and the scholarly
kind, case-hardened in tyranny.

Then in the bloody domain of the flies
The United Fruit Company Incorporated
unloaded with a booty of coffee and fruits
brimming its cargo boats, gliding

like trays with the spoils
of our drowning dominions.

And all the while, somewhere, in the sugary
hells of our seaports,
smothered by gases, an Indian
fell in the morning:
a body spun off, an anonymous
chattel, some numeral tumbling,
a branch with its death running out of it
in the vat of the carrion, fruit laden and foul.

Translated by Ben Belitt

Hoeing

GARY SOTO *United States*

During March while hoeing long rows
Of cotton
Dirt lifted in the air
Entering my nostrils
And eyes
The yellow under my fingernails

The hoe swung
Across my shadow   chopping weeds
And thick caterpillars
That shriveled
Into rings
And went where the wind went

When the sun was on the left
And against my face
Sweat   the sea
That is still within me
Rose and fell from my chin
Touching land
For the first time

Farm Labourer

GEORGE MACKAY BROWN *Scotland*

"God, am I not dead yet?" said Ward, his ear
Meeting another dawn.
   A blackbird, lost in leaves, began to throb
And on the pier
   The gulls stretched barbarous throats
   Over the creels, the haddock lines, the boats.
His mortal pain
   All day hung tangled in that lyrical web.
"Seventy years I've had of this," said Ward,
"Going in winter dark
   To feed the horse, a lantern in my fist,
Snow in my beard,
   Then thresh in the long barn
   Bread and ale out of the skinflint corn,
And such-like work!"
   And a lark flashed its needle down the west.

Cattle

KIJIMA HAJIME *Japan*

There flows
the enormous conveyor belt.
The driven black masses are lured out,
cornered into the cold granite mouth.
How sticky is the snivel
dripping incessantly from their nostrils!
The gloomiest rumbles, groans, and commotion come
as from the very bottom of a deluge.
Clusters of shiny black horns thrust skyward from time to time
like the knives of angry children,
some tossed up like a mass of driftwood against the shore.
Even their sexual excitement is a desperate protest!
Shoved back and forth, they jump and bend over one another,
bulls, steers, cows, and oxen.
They cannot see or bite off halters.
The rows of their black backs flow
so irritatingly slowly
toward the slaughterhouse.
Like a flooded river
the herds of black cattle flow endlessly
toward the iron fences of the slaughterer.

Translated by Naoshi Koriyama and Edward Lueders

Sugar Cane

FAUSTIN CHARLES *Great Britain*

The succulent flower bleeds molasses,
as its slender, sweet stalks bend,
beheaded in the breeze.

The green fields convulse golden sugar,
tossing the rain aside,
out-growing the sun,
and carving faces
in the sun-sliced panorama.

The reapers come at noon,
riding the cutlass-whip;
their saliva sweetens everything
in the boiling season.

Each stem is a flashing arrow,
swift in the harvest.

Cane is sweet sweat slain;
cane is labour, unrecognized, lost
and unrecovered;
sugar is the sweet swollen pain of the years;
sugar is slavery's immovable stain;
cane is water lying down,
and water standing up.

Cane is a slaver;
cane is bitter,
very bitter,
in the sweet blood of life.

The Sugar Slave

THYLIAS MOSS *United States*

Once upon a time a little boy felled a tree
that nobody heard in the Dominican Republic or
in Haiti where he was purchased for what usually
is an hour's wage in Texas and everywhere north
that has these lovely crystal jars, crafted
to catch light in ways that exaggerate breakfast,
filled with sugar, perhaps Domino brand (Freudianly
named for a certain effect), perhaps not, but likely
from the forest of cane the boy chopped down.

> *He must therefore be superhuman.*
> *He must therefore live in a fairy tale.* Why

the machete is as long as his legs! He's
only eight. By the time he is thirty-eight
his legs will be much longer, but the machete
will be bigger than his life.

> *This therefore is miraculous.*
> *This therefore remains a fairy tale.*

From the poorest island he has been snatched
into comparative paradise, Dominican paradise.
So, so sweet an opportunity. He will have a room
and six others will have it too. And he will have
all the cane (and only cane) he can eat and eat and
he cannot possibly eat it all. He will have no toilet
(not that he ever did); the pee will snake
through the cane which will be even sweeter.

> *Therefore the cane is enchanted.*
> *Therefore this is a fairy tale.*

The boy gleams in his sweat like the knight cutting
through thicket and briars to wake at precisely

the right moment the one getting her beauty sleep
or she wouldn't be beautiful, a cake, too soon
from the oven, that although young droops and sags
like the old woman no one wants to become, a cake
with the sugar extracted, with silicon substitutes
and other lifts, tucks, and preservatives.

   Therefore mirror mirror hype.
   Therefore mirror mirror hope.

The boy cuts through miles and years of cane.
When something is as beautiful as the promise
the sun makes every morning when the cane
seems a garden of golden flagpoles marking independence,
end of colonialism, he would try to kiss it if
his mouth had not been ruined. He bites deep
into the raw form.

   He bites the fairy tale in two.

He bites into what hypnosis wants to take you to
so you can understand hatred denied, repressed,
refined and in the jar you pass upon request.

Summer

BINYO IVANOV *Bulgaria*

On this long farm facing Rila Mountain,
filled with tobacco carts,
my father's grave is ripening.
On this long farm facing Rila Mountain
where the sun bathes twenty villages
with twenty houses each,
where the river that had set out for fish
disappears at the edge of a melon field.
The hills head east,
three dry shrubs on their foreheads,
they're thinking of becoming mountains;
on their wide way
my father's grave is ripening.

His friends have forgotten him,
mother's forgotten him
and I'll forget him soon —
but the sun looks on,
the tobacco grows sturdy and bitter,
the melons puff themselves up,
soon a colorful ant
will emerge from the slab
and say, "It's ripe now!"
In a while the market will be laden with
heaps of tapped and chiming melons
and bulging tobacco bales,

and the hills, their foreheads blazing,
will keep on heading east.

Translated by Lisa Sapinkopf

They Plow

GIOVANNI PASCOLI *Italy*

In the field, where russet in the row
some tendril shines, and from thickets
morning mist seems to smoke,

They plow: with slow command, one drives
slow cows; others sow; one strikes
ridges with his hoe patiently;

'cause the knowing sparrow's heart already rejoices,
and he spies on everything from bristling branches of mulberry;
and the robin: in hedges is heard
his tinkling, fine as gold.

Translated by Marc Wolterbeek

Farmer

JACK MYERS *United States*

He counted himself no different
from the rain driving on
the houses, melting down
the stiff lives rocking
in their attics.
When his anger nailed up
the house too small and tight
he would grab for the hard
candies and close his hand
around his son's.

He remembered the helplessness
of a black hawk beating upwards
being jabbed by a faster bird;
how his second-hand bed
still held the broad shape
of another man. He tried hard
because the dirt did.
He knew his rest was coming
from a long way off
and what great thing shone
inside it, he figured, was him.

Pears

MARY SWANDER *United States*

Dipping each nail
in grease, she hammers
a porch around her house
so no one will see her
come or go, but I
stand here knocking,
the sun pouring
through the glass,
my back warm as the flame
in the stove she keeps
burning summer and
winter to drive
away evil. And no one
sees her slip through
the door, the walls
like sod, holding out
the heat, the rain,
and no one answers
my call as she slides
deeper into the far
room. She leaves
her shoes on the cellar
stairs and the mud-caked
soles dry into
their own faces,
dry into the shape
of the pears rotting
on the shelf. The light
fades into the wall,
into the cistern filling
with sand and stone.
The light fades
into the fence posts,
clothesline,
the heartwood of the pear

tree fallen down
behind the shed,
there to be chopped
for the stove inside,
there, where for days
I stand in her shoes
with an axe and do not
feel the rain, do not
hear the blossoms forming,
do not see them burn white
deep inside the walls
of their own stems.

West Texas

LANGSTON HUGHES *United States*

Down in West Texas where the sun
Shines like the evil one
I had a woman
And her name
Was Joe.

Pickin' cotton in the field
Joe said I wonder how it would feel
For us to pack up
Our things
And go?

So we cranked up our old Ford
And we started down the road
Where we was goin'
We didn't know —
Nor which way.

But West Texas where the sun
Shines like the evil one
Ain't no place
For a colored
Man to stay!

Ploughman

JOHN TRIPP *Wales*

"You may not get a chance
to see this again," the correspondent
from Power Farming said to me.

Near Builth I watched him
slowly carve up a plot
in neat straight grooves, doing
a precision high-cut run
with the polished furrow slices
gleaming like metal.
He turned through an exact angle
of a hundred-and-thirty degrees
without breaking, and packing firm
against the previous slice.
It was the true straightness
of the lines you had to see,
as if he steered along white paint.

The shires stopped on a tuppence
when he yelled Whoa!
They stopped with one foot in the air
and put it back, not forward.
He fussed and tuned his ship
when he felt a slight change
of texture, or the horses leaned
into a breeze. He did an acre
a day, walking ten miles
behind the big patient team.
A really bad error was visible
in soil or crop for a year.
His craft seemed timeless, and beautiful.

He was one of the last
of his skill. I'm glad I saw it
before his plough went to a museum.

Muddy Road to Adam Johnson's House

after Andrew Wyeth

JOHN BURNSIDE *Scotland*

It's this knowing the land by the names
of neighbors: the long-deceased
and the newborn; the tactful farm-wives
standing in their yards; the hedges and orchards
grubbed out years ago, lit in the mind
with ghost rain fuzzing the leaves;

and, under it all, the pure geography
of childhood walks and first snow and the time
you stopped at Kuerner's barn to warm your hands
and saw a young buck, pouring from the roof,
the ankles crossed, the last thick cloud of steam
hanging around the muzzle and the groin

and this was the heat you breathed
in the first chill of winter.

Winter Journey

UWE-MICHAEL GUTZSCHHAHN *Germany*

And I think
to travel in this winter light's
perhaps better than nothing
the fields glide past outside
the ploughed land frozen hard
beneath the thin snow
the shades of landscape
paler almost mild
broad the dormant expanses
from wayside cross to wayside cross
traces
as if in fact there were still trees
with a bench beneath them
and above starlings fly
from their wooden boxes

The Old Vineyard

LEONARDO SINISGALLI *Italy*

I've been sitting on the ground
beside the haystack in the old vineyard.
Children pull nuts from the branches
and crush them between two stones.
My hands are messy with green slime.
I savor the air coming from the heart of the trees.

Translated by W. S. Di Piero

A Pair of Shoes by the Field's Edge

WANG XIANI *China*

By the field's edge
A pair of cloth shoes neatly stand
To which hardworking man do they belong?
Maybe he wants only to stick closer to earth?
— Sounds of hoes working the fields
Swaths of green, gleaming corn greet the eyes.

All corn stalks are sturdy
And they'll surely bear corn, the like of gold nuggets.
That pair of cloth shoes still looks new
With fine, neat stitches.
— Over there who is
Booming out snatches of opera tunes?

As the whistle sounds for a break,
A young man dashes out of the field,
Stout, proper and very handsome.
The sun looks like his giant earring,
— He laughs, he shouts, he jumps around,
"My precious shoes are still over there."

Tapping away the dust on his shoes,
Then taking a look at his muddy feet,
He tucks the shoes under his arm.
The road is smoldering hot under the sun.
Thump, thump, thump,
Bare feet trudging on earth, the color of antique bronze.

At a Potato Digging

SEAMUS HEANEY *Ireland*

I

A mechanical digger wrecks the drill,
Spins up a dark shower of roots and mould.
Labourers swarm in behind, stoop to fill
Wicker creels. Fingers go dead in the cold.

Like crows attacking crow-black fields, they stretch
A higgledy line from hedge to headland;
Some pairs keep breaking ragged ranks to fetch
A full creel to the pit and straighten, stand

Tall for a moment but soon stumble back
To fish a new load from the crumbled surf.
Heads bow, trunks bend, hands fumble towards the black
Mother. Processional stooping through the turf

Recurs mindlessly as autumn. Centuries
Of fear and homage to the famine god
Toughen the muscles behind their humbled knees,
Make a seasonal altar of the sod.

II

Flint-white, purple. They lie scattered
like inflated pebbles. Native
to the black hutch of clay
where the halved seed shot and clotted
these knobbed and slit-eyed tubers seem
the petrified hearts of drills. Split
by the spade, they show white as cream.

Good smells exude from crumbled earth.
The rough bark of humus erupts

knots of potatoes (a clean birth)
whose solid feel, worse wet inside
promises taste of ground and root.
To be piled in pits; live skulls, blind-eyed.

III

Live skulls, blind-eyed, balanced on
wild higgledy skeletons
scoured the land in 'forty-five,
wolfed the blighted root and died.

The new potato, sound as stone,
putrefied when it had lain
three days in the long clay pit.
Millions rotted along with it.

Mouths tightened in, eyes died hard,
faces chilled to a plucked bird.
In a million wicker huts
beaks of famine snipped at guts.

A people hungering from birth,
grubbing, like plants, in the bitch earth,
were grafted with a great sorrow.
Hope rotted like a marrow.

Stinking potatoes fouled the land,
pits turned pus into filthy mounds:
and where potato diggers are
you still smell the running sore.

IV

Under a gay flotilla of gulls
The rhythm deadens, the workers stop.

Brown bread and tea in bright canfuls
Are served for lunch. Dead-beat, they flop

Down in the ditch and take their fill,
Thankfully breaking timeless fasts;
Then, stretched on the faithless ground, spill
Libations of cold tea, scatter crusts.

Faces at the First Farmworkers' Constitutional Convention

JOSÉ MONTOYA *United States*

Just the other day
In Fresno
In a giant arena
Architectured
To reject the very poor
Cesar Chavez brought
The very poor
Together
In large numbers.

Cuatrocientos delegados
On the convention floor
Alone
And a few
Thousand more
In the galleries —

And outside
(. . . parecia el mercado
    de Toluca!)

The very poor had come
Together
For protection —

Thousands
From the chaos
Of past shameful harvests
Culminating

That humble man's
Awesome task
Of organizing
The unorganizables!

Farmworkers!
(Workers of the fields!)

Campesinos!
(Peones de los campos de
    labores!)

Not lifeless executives.
Not, stranger yet,
Pompous politicians!

What I saw
Were the familiar
Faces
Of yester grapes
And labor camps.

Body dragging faces
Baked in the oven
Valle de Coachella
And frost blistered
En las heladas de Sanger
During pruning time.

Faces that have
Dealt with
Exploiters and
Deporters
Y con contratistas
Chuecos.

Faces!

Faces black
From Florida with love
And Coca Cola

Y Raza
De Chicago
Brown Brown
y de Tejas
y Arabes de Lamont
y Filipinos de Delano
y así gente
That had come
From all the fields
Of all the farmlands
Of America

Farmworkers!
Campesinos!
The very poor!
The unorganizables —
Now, at a convention!

Yet,
No fancy vinyl-covered
Briefcases here,
No Samsonite luggage
Or Botany 500s,

Solo ropa del trabajo
Pero bien planchadita
Y portafolios sencillos
De cartón
Y cada quien con su
Mochilita
Y taquitos
En el parking lot

Where old acquaintances
Renew friendships

And compare the
Different experiences
Of late

No longer merely
Comparing wages and
Camp conditions like
Before . . .
        (. . . a cuanto andan
            pagando
        pa' ya pa' la costa?)

New queries now, reflecting
The different experiences
Of late . . .

        (. . . and how many times
            were
        you arrested, brother?)

And the talk of the market
Place continues
And they listen to
Boastful, seasoned travelers
Who have left, for the time
Being, at least,
The well-worn routes
Of the harvest followers
And they talk of
Strange sounding places . . .

        (. . . pos sabe que yo andaba
        en el boicoteo pa' ya pa'
        filadelfia.)

The talk of the market place
The parking place
The market lot
The parking lot

Where the families
Were bedded down
For three days
Amidst amistad
Y canciones

Canciones y mas canciones
Singing de colores,
About solidaridad
Pa' siempre
And we shall overcome
En Español

Singing, singing . . .

Componiendo corridos
To freeze in time and space
The events
Of that struggle . . .

   Año del '73
   Presente lo tengo yo
   De aquella infame cosecha
   Y el triunfo de nuestra unión

   Ay valle de San Joaquín
   Campo santo de mi gente
   Porque nos tratas tan mal
   Como hijos desobedientes

And they sang of injustice and
   they sang
Of broken promises . . .

   Los chotas también decian
   Que no querian violencia
   Pero eran puras habladas
   Maltrataban sin conciencia

Y mesclaban los versos de risa
   y los de valor . . .

   No desfiaba un ranchero
   Un esquirol y su abuela
   Pero nuestro entrenamiento
   Fue en el valle de Coachella

Corridos serios and at times
   irreverent . . .

   En eso cambio el asunto
   Y empezaron arrestar
   Echanron corte parejo
   No habia pa' donde
      arrancar

   Perdoname Cesar Chavez
   Y la Virgen Guadalupe
   Pero antes de que me
      arresten

   Los voy' hacer que se
      preocupen

And always they sang of
   hope . . .

   Ay díganle a mi cuadrilla
   Y a la oficina de Selma
   Que no rompan mi tarjeta
   Que ay les caigo pa' la cena

Even inside
On that floor of decorum
Singing
In defiance
Of Mr. Robert's own rules!

Singing
Singing and joking

(. . . el que esté en acuerdo
con mi moción, que me
la apele!)

Ca ca car ca ja das
And table pounding
Belly rolls

Then
Earnestly, without
    embarrassment
Back to work.
Faces!
Faces de farmworkers —
Organized!
Confident!
Unafraid!

Resoluteness
without impudence —

(. . . me dispensa hermano
    director,
pero mi gente no
    ha comido.)

Faces!

Faces de campesinos,
Faces of the very poor,
Confident,
Unafraid —

The unorganizables,
The people of the earth —
La gente de la tierra
Today
Very seriously
Contemplating
The ratification
Of Article 37
For history
And forever!

The Hill Farmer Speaks

R. S. THOMAS *Wales*

I am the farmer, stripped of love
And thought and grace by the land's hardness;
But what I am saying over the fields'
Desolate acres, rough with dew,
Is, Listen, listen, I am a man like you.

The wind goes over the hill pastures
Year after year, and the ewes starve,
Milkless, for want of the new grass.
And I starve, too, for something the spring
Can never foster in veins run dry.

The pig is a friend, the cattle's breath
Mingles with mine in the still lanes;
I wear it willingly like a cloak
To shelter me from your curious gaze.

The hens go in and out at the door
From sun to shadow, as stray thoughts pass
Over the floor of my wide skull.
The dirt is under my cracked nails;
The tale of my life is smirched with dung;
The phlegm rattles. But what I am saying
Over the grasses rough with dew
Is, Listen, listen, I am a man like you.

Legacy

MÁRTON KALÁSZ *Hungary*

I don't see my mother dancing —
in my thoughts she still trims vines
sprayed blue with copper sulfate
for her two bags of wheat, eight bushels rye.
I don't know if her young face
was lovely, if the other tenants
admired her dragonfly form,
or if my blond father tethered his horse only
at our cabin in the wild Whitsun ride.
I just see her in the wintry dawn
chopping cornstalks at the stove
or patching sacks in the stilled yard;
I see her at evening in the vineyard
secretly taking flowers for my dead father.
Such memories pour into me,
and whirl me round fiercely now —
my mother, whom none could help,
in the darkness of whose flesh
the cancer spread its deadly arms,
who left her son this legacy.
This is not to blame her, not one curse
ever left her lips, I know . . . Only, poverty
took it all from her vein-roped hands.
Half a day she walked to find me, a hand
at some far-off farm, bringing me potatoes she spared,
spending her scant saving on my studies;
and when I scanned my first lines
at the window something silvery
glowed in her eyes — joy.
And then she was gone, never to see
the first book. I could thrust no money
secretly beneath her bolster, for a dress, for salt —
her bones in the graveyard
moldered to fat silent clay; now flowers force their roots
in summer where her forehead used to be.

And I carry her legacy for good:
on my face the mark of sorrow,
in myself humility's soundless load;
until I die I shall not forget
that world of grinding poverty —
in the field we are walking
like yoked horses together forever.

Translated by Jascha Kessler

III

In a Fallow Field in the North

Conversation at Midnight

ADELINA ADALIS *Russia*

One of midnight's charms is a muted terror —
Beside the river at the Burnoye Farm,
Kardanakhi wine from Georgia
Loosens tongues.
With bated breath, like kids,
We sat in the weakly guttering light
On mattresses of straw
With glasses in our hands,
And the wind blew softly bluish-pink
Reflected off the roses.
And the director of our group of farms
Began to speak. His voice was strange:

"Listen to the river moving, sighing,
Smell the laurels, smell the reeds.
Every human being has
A hidden corner in his soul.
In the spirit's golden mists,
In the moist warmth of that abyss
Live only the glimmers of his desires
And the passions they conceal.
Anyone can swank or boast,
But we're not at a District Council now,
Let each of us confess this once
About our hopes and what we treasure."

The local frontier force commander
Began. He told us of his days of sadness
"When my old bones begin to ache
In the long fall days and when
I find my temples graying fast.
I remember pleading once for love
And being crushed by a refusal.
The young woman whom then I loved
Still seems to me to be endowed with wings.

69

From our army camp we look out
On nothing but dull emptiness.
On sultry nights the trumpeter
Breaks young hearts by sounding taps . . .
Not nightingales but the croak of frogs
Shatters the night in different tones,
While that graceful maiden endowed with wings
Had tresses of an orange-gold.
The horses in our camp are scared,
The thickly rising dust burns hot,
But graceful maiden endowed with wings,
With your soft pink flanks you could
Have floated through that camp of ours,
Like clouds in spring."

He fell silent and deeply saddened,
Gazed toward the river landing
Where empty rafts knocked against each other . . .
But the farm economist replied:
"No, it's not by figures or the balance sheet,
Nor by the percentage of births of calves,
Whereby we take the measure of our lives.
Be it on business or be it in argument,
But long ago I came to love
The solitary playing of a flute
And the gentle sobbing of a violin.
I remember once, an evening in a square,
The reservoir abrim with nasturtiums,
Guarneri's festive violin,
Singing Schubert's 'Geh'n wir,'
Like a righteous man who after death
Finds himself on the azure bank.
I was at the concert with a girl
And still I can't forget it all . . ."

. . . In contemplation and delight,
Maintaining his slow air of pride,
He began to pace the hall
While the frontier commander asked of me,

"You, young fellow, seem to be
Cock-a-hoop at these confessions;
Children and fools are told many things
About you. People say strange things of you.
You're not a child to've made no errors.
To hell with lies, to hell with cant.
Tell us about those things
That you hold most sacred in your mind."

I told them this: "You're right, of course.
In my final hour of life,
I want still to be able to
Pick out Kardanakhi from Tsinandali
And someone beautiful from all the rest.
I'm not a child — I've made mistakes —
I'm not indebted to either of you;
I shall tell you the most tender thing
That I hold sacred in my mind . . .
Walking once through Moscow's streets
With March's ice smelling slightly sweet,
A tinge of vodka or sour cherries . . .
It was evening, with a gentle frost,
But all along Kuznetsky Most
Sprigs of mimosa were on sale.
I remember all those signs of bliss
That for me overflowed the brim;
I remember that in the special editions
It said that Shanghai'd been taken by the South.
When shall such times come again?
I remember taking back to my room
A veritable orchard of mimosa
And a liter of table wine from the barrel,
Inviting home three of my friends as well,
To read the papers while the mimosa sprays
Threw shadows on the ceiling.
Who could have thought then of betrayal?
My wretched city, you're so far off,
May my own grave punish me
Should I ever dare forget you.

Oh, how distant is that happiness
And how that memory still hurts me."
I screamed the words out and would not dare
Ever repeat what then I said —
The blushing flush of shame
Crawled red across my cheeks and brow —
The bitterness of unclean tenderness
Of immoderate passion's flame! . . .
My two bosom friends, embarrassed,
Stepped away from me in shock.

I walked off alone a little,
Swearing softly at myself.

The captain ran out after me,
Grabbed me by the sleeve and said:
"So, you've confessed. So you've had it bad.
But listen to an old man talking.
It's difficult to spit things out,
But let's be sincere to the bitter end.
I begged for love in tears, I tell you,
While the dark clouds swirled and rose.

"There's a maiden endowed with wings,
The color of light and milk and honey.
But we have many enemies among us
Seeking ID papers and a corner.
That woman came to my bedside
And spoke to me as to a child,
'Life is soft and life is sweet,'
But I rose and threw her out
From the army camp I lived in.
Sometimes life is hard to us.
We know passion, but also fear.
But the moment that's decisive
Always finds us at our posts.
And my real love lies here before you
From the subtropics to the tundra.

I bear its symbol on my breast,
But I cannot talk freely of it;
Better to put up with any torment
Than offend the one we love.
That's what I think . . . Give me your hand,
Let us smile but be silent."

But the director then grew angry,
"Is it only you with a right to joy?
Brothers, I learned stage by stage
String music and slow words.
A violin made merry in my room,
A girl sang, the food got cold . . .
On my Fergana bed covers
Fell a pinkish twilight glow.
Amid this soft sweet darkened gloom
The festive winter long drew out
Till one day a letter came
Written in an uncouth hand:

"'In these parts in bitter truth
Where we've plowed down to the river,
We have no calico, no silk brocade,
All our bulls are old and idle,
But on this farm, in this climate
We could make things different now.
In these parts in nineteen-twenty
You were wounded in the chest.
Ready to meet an honorable death
You lay here on a sheaf of grass,
So your blood is truly mingled
In this country with our soil.'

"Then I set off across the snowy steppes,
Smoking in a railway coach,
And don't recall what else I did,
What I said to my train companions,
What then I thought I've since forgotten:

"The fickle winds blew it away.
I kissed the blackened cheeks
Of a shepherd I'd never seen before.
Sometimes life goes dead against us.
We know passion, we know fear,
But the moment that's decisive
Always finds us at our posts.
And my true love lies here before us
From the subtropics to the tundra.
I bear its banner in my hands
But I cannot talk about it freely . . .
We are warmed by hidden tenderness.
Don't think me a pious fool.
These Party Members' cards of ours
Will someday become breathing people.
It's better to put up with any torment
Than offend the one we love.
That's what I think . . . Give me your hand.

"Let's smile with joy and fall silent
And clumsy, perhaps, but hand in hand.
How joyous can be sincerity."
We stood there as the weak lamp flickered
On the undecorated table
And westward below the escarpment slope,
At a place where three roads met
Our young settlement continued sleeping
In a silent trustfulness.
And beneath the hill that lay to eastward,
Horses snorted, watchdogs barked.
The peaceful new buildings slept
Along the frontier demarcation line
And up their walls and on their roofs
Rolled a golden wave of mist:
It seemed to us it was being breathed
By coal miners and by fishermen.
And the azure night flowed by us
Over shimmering clouds of human warmth.

Translated by Bernard Meares

74

Red Beard

NUALA ARCHER *Panama*

Travelling
porous
towards
Spring
on
this
membrane
of
5
billion
people
honeycombed
into
inextinguishable
centuries
your
face
surfaces
reborn
reddened
with
my
breathing
blood.

In a Fallow Field in the North
Is a Plow That Hurts Me

DUO DUO *China*

In a fallow field in the north is a plow that hurts me.
When spring lies down like a horse, from an
Empty carriage for collecting corpses
A head made of stone
Gathers storms of death.

The steel hair of the storm that brushes
Against the hat
Is emptiness — the time after death
Has taken off his face:
A brown beard stretches forward
To gather the dignity long fallow in the north.

Spring is like the bell gnawing at his heart,
Like the sound of a child's head sinking under the water in a well,
Like a child being boiled over a fire.
His pain is like a giant

Sawing lumber
As if sawing his own leg —
A sound weaker than sadness
Threading through the sawmill where work has stopped,
Through the lonely storerooms.
It's the loneliness of a sower walking to the end of the field.

A flax-colored peasant woman
Waves her hand although she has no face,
Waves at the bent back of a plowman.
An improficient mother has no memory,
But she waves — like a stone
From a distant ancestor.

Translated by Michelle Yeh

Depths of Fields

LUIS CABALQUINTO *Philippines*

I walk some hundred paces from the old house
where I was raised, where many are absent now,

and the rice fields sweep into view: there where
during home leaves I'm drawn to watch on evenings

such as this, when the moon is fat and much given
to the free spending of its rich cache of light

which transmutes all things: it changes me now,
like someone restored to the newness of his life.

Note the wind's shuffle in the crown of tall coconut
trees; the broad patches of moon-flecked water —

freshly-rowed with seedlings; the grass huts of
croppers, windows framed by the flicker of kerosene

lamps: an unearthly calm pervades all that is seen.
Beauty unreserved holds down a country's suffering.

Disclosed in this high-pitched hour: a long-held
secret displayed by ambition and need, a country

boy's pained enchantment with his hometown lands
that remains intact in a lifetime of wanderings.

As I look again, embraced by depths of an old
loneliness, I'm permanently returned to this world,

to the meanings it has saved for me. If I die now,
in the grasp of childhood fields, I'll miss nothing.

The Spring

Korea 1951

P. J. KAVANAGH *Ireland*

The paper house was empty in the middle of the paddy
So we took it over. The electricians
Fixed up some wiring; we had a crate of
Guinness in the lorry; we'd come a long way
But first we must get settled.
The partitions, the rooms, were small. The locals were small,
But the owner must have been a man of some substance,
There were plenty of rooms, and the house miles from nowhere.
Soon there were yellow bulbs swinging from black flex;
All had their quarters; a dry-patch for the lorries . . .
Then somebody smelled the burning.
Something wrong with the wiring.
Up to our anklets in mud
We watched it burn down, drinking Guinness.
Nothing for it now but put up tents on the dry-patch.
A man floated face downward in the mud.
There were helmets and webbing equipment we didn't
Inquire under. Now there was kerosene
In the tents, and wooden duck-walks.

In front of the smouldering house,
In the shallow pond where the man lay,
Was a bubble of spring; in the morning
We went there to wash. It was warm.
Out of the earth, dribbling on to the mud
Between two stones, came a spring that was warm.
We used it to shave in; while around,
Women patiently gathered with their washing:
The people whose blessing it was
Waiting for us to go.

Downstream

LINDA HUSSA *United States*

In that house across the field they accommodate God's will
on a blackboard by the back door, a psalm to start the day or
    end it,
to accept the portion dealt from life's unlevel spoon. Their land
    is dry
unless the upstream neighbor, owning first flow rights,
turns water out all winter, lets his ditches freeze in wells above
    the ice,
to hold and hold, to overflow beyond his fields
where water doesn't know that fences have a name. Then his
    meadows
fresh with flood, the dormant seeds will split the skin, radicle and
    cotyledon
worm down and up to dark and light — all things making use
    of both,
the blackboard keeps them mindful of. The ground will dole out
    moisture
to satisfy the root, to flesh the leaf, to fill the sleeve. A simple man,
his needs are just: pasturage for his cows, a bait of decent food
to feed his rough-cheeked children gathered 'round the kitchen
    stove
with books, and toys and handwork. The rooms are small and
    don't ask
much wood to heat them. The pines he planted as a lad
keep snows from shouldering up the walls. He fills his plate
with beef he raised, picks his teeth with gratitude
for his neighbor's greed that gives him yet another year.

But last winter the upstream neighbor turned the ditch, let it flood
the channel, let it carry to the lake because he tired of cleaning out
forgotten toys of summer and paper sacks and weeds
that dammed the culverts, and damned him when townsfolk
drew their miseries out in one long breath. He took his share in
    spring

but not enough to cross the land and reach the man downstream.
  Then summer
took its turn and no rain fell except in numbers he could count like
  stones
across the road. The meadow parched, blew off in dust. The pond
  cracked open.
Moans of drought shook above the ground in waves. He pumped
the house-well to keep the orchard living. The towering
  cottonwoods
around the house put out leaves like lilac, small and cupped to
  gather dew
and by the first of August reached grey bones of branches
  clattering in the winds.
He weaned calves as light as leppies to save the cows from falling
  off.
The blackboard was rubbed clean and in its blankness was the
  prophet.
The neighbor hoards the sin of ignorance. The believer lives
  downstream.

July 2nd, 1916

'British Attack on The Somme'

PHOEBE HESKETH *Great Britain*

Six o'clock reveille: Scamblers Farm
and a shotgun bolt withdrawn.
Thump on the trestle, the first pig is landed
twisting, screaming; overhead
fantails murmur soft as down
while these, necklaced fine and red
under the accurate knife,
are bubbling, gargling gouts of blood
congealing to rubies
on glistening cobbles and boots.

On my seventh birthday, torn
from a feathered dream, I awake
to nightmare loud and warm
trampling the summer air,
and I'm running, head down, through the gate
shielded by trees to the river.

R. F. D. Mailbox

S. A. WALSH *United States*

Red Barn Perspective

I was haven
and workplace,
shelter
and delivery room.
I was sustenance
to the world.

I waited
through generations
of lambs.
Listened
as tinkling cowbells
led the way
to the shelter.

R. F. D. Perspective

Eager, happy,
hope-filled hands
reached for me.
Sad, broken-hearted
trembling hands
shook me slightly.
Strong backs,
weakened by the
news I carried
leaned against me.
Giggles and laughter
trickled over me as
young lovers
exchanged vows

through me.
I am the only one
who remembers.
I am their
sole monument.

Fat of the Land

GEORGIANA VALOYCE-SANCHEZ *United States*

Walking to public school
beyond the housing project compound
I would ponder the "fat
of the land"
What it meant
Why my folks always talked
about it

When there was nothing left to eat
but beans   Steinbeck
would appear at our table
blowing smoke rings with his big
cigar and he'd lean back in our
rickety kitchen chair and talk
about the "fat
of the land"

When I got older with babies and
two cars in my suburban garage
my folks went back home
to Indian land
Reservation   rocks broken bottle glass
an old shack in the foothills
of the San Gorgonio's
    and I asked them
is this it Is this
It?
Where's the fat?
And my father would lean back against
a scrawny birch   blow smoke rings
with his clay pipe   and smile

I had to admit
the handful of pale pink strawberries
he had coaxed from the stony ground

were the   sweetest
I had ever tasted
and there was no denying
the singing that took place
when my mother and father knelt
to pat the earth
beneath the bare peach tree

In Peru, the Quechans Have a
Thousand Words for Potato

RAY GONZÁLEZ *Peru*

I hold my cut finger to the ice water,
return from the source of grain in the teeth —
the country where I knew a thousand words for love,

a handful of eye movements, not knowing
which direction to take, which roots to dig
and pile among vegetables.

In Peru, they open their hands,
offer the potato as the fruit from the top of the world,
people who fled the mountains for a crop at lower depths,

descending to cut the potato and find
the white meat, fiber tasting like the grain
that gave them speech.

Their vowels make me wish
I had a thousand words by my body,
a vegetable and tree planted from the testicle,

the black spot in the potato named
for the thousand sons, limbs holding up
the back of the tired worker,

strangers who eat with their fingers and go back
to the high fields for the potato given
the thousand and one name,

dug from the soil they slept on,
the field where they paused to piss
before climbing up the mountain.

Stomping the Beaver Palace

ROGER WEINGARTEN *United States*

Water flows down the mountain
into a clawfoot tub in the cellar,
where I circle a skunk curled up
in the furnace and a half-blind
vole feasting on a plate
of poisoned wheat. Sometimes
the water pipe jutting
out of fieldstone seizes
up in winter, sometimes the World
War II water heater pilot
blows itself out, or I get the urge
to watch the groundthaw in April
purl into a sump pump
buried in the coal-studded floor,
scrape my skull against a square-head nail
pounded into a beam a century
and a half ago by the farmer who hollowed
out a future in unobliging soil
and aim my flashlight into the crawlspace,
where a predator made a furious meal
of a mourning dove. I crawl in
and twig to how it feels to orbit
a planet in a tin can. From this eye socket
perch, I press my palm to the light
like a fortuneteller revealing the red-
shadowed future of my bones, turn it off
to see myself in the dark execute
a buck and wing on the mud-and-stick
tiled roof of a beaver palace, then slap
and dive toward the entrance
into the catacomb. Upstairs, and still
bristling at my refusal to attend
courses in synchronized
breathing and belly-dancing, my wife

spears the blackened remnants
out of the toaster, our child,
upside-down and floating
inside her, ready to scream.

Quail and His Role in Agriculture

RAY A. YOUNG BEAR *United States*

"Now it's here
that time which
was once forthcoming
for us to remember
our older/younger brother
Quail," was how I composed
a song for John Louis.
Though I had very little
to do with him socially
or the family way,
ever since my cousin
acknowledged his unrequited
love fifteen years ago,
I thought it befitting
to present this song
to him before the next
memorial.

As I began to drum on the car's
dashboard with my fingers,
several horticulturalists
who were waiting their turn
at the Tastee Freez line
looked my way. Their clothes
were resplendent: bright baseball
caps with fertilizer logos,
ironed overalls, and new workshirts;
but their faces were tired and expression-
less. With the constant drone of harvesting
machinery in their ears, they probably
thought the tapping was yet another
mechanical trouble to contend with,
for they were the only ones to turn
their heads. The rest just wanted
to order.

It was a hot September day, and we
had all stopped to have strawberry
sundaes: I, to celebrate my song;
and they, to soothe the grain and dust
in their throats. Midwesterners, all,
standing in the monolithic shadow
of a hydraulic platform, which lifted
the semi-truck's cab to the sky
to violently shake and dislodge
its cargo of yellow corn —
the historic sustenance
which was now to some
a symbol of abject poverty.
For others, like myself and all
my grandfathers before me, it continues
to be a transmitter of prayer.
Beautiful yellow corn . . .

Sprout

RUMIKO KŌRA *Japan*

When I discovered
that the Japanese for "sprout"
was written with "crown of grass" on top of "tusk"
I imagined a sprout appearing from the ground
breaking through the frozen air.

Men of old must have gotten discouraged
roaming the mountains all day long
not finding a single wild boar or deer
no doubt they'd hunted them all down
a family can't live on rabbits and birds alone.

They must have seen a field one day
where women were growing potatoes,
with its rows of curved sprouts
gleaming like polished white tusks.

"These are our tusks," they must have thought
so they made the character for "sprout"
with a crown of grass atop a tusk
and declared the sprouts were theirs
because those who make the words rule the world.

In a woman's illusory field
invisible sprouts keep
breaking through the frozen earth
their fresh tusks appearing from the ground
not to tear, but to yield.

Translated by Leza Lowitz and Miyuki Aoyama

The Dead Calf

RICHARD JONES *United States*

Snow has fallen,
and a mournful lowing
drifts through a slate-gray mist,

bringing the farmer
puttering into clarity
with his son on a slow blue tractor.

The machine idles
as the boy jumps down
and strikes the cow with a stick,

whipping her
to the edge of the field,
where she calls across the pasture

as her heavy calf is carted away
in the baling arms of the tractor.

Pastoral

RONALD WALLACE *United States*

They say it was an absence of cows
that brought this old barn down,
twisted the stone foundation
against itself until the king beams,
swaybacked and woozy, cracked under
the strain of so much dry air.
Moisture, our neighbor farmer,
leaning back on his heels, said. *Moisture*

and heat would have saved it. Sweet
Jesus! What must it take,
in these late days of our ransacked
lives, to save what's left of longings
on which we put everything down?
Who'll off to market, singing *cows, cows*?

November Calf

JANE KENYON *United States*

She calved in the ravine, beside
the green-scummed pond.
Full clouds and mist hung low —
it was unseasonably warm. Steam
rose from her head as she pushed
and called; her cries went out
over the still-lush fields.

First came the front feet, then
the blossom-nose, shell-pink
and glistening; and then the broad
forehead, flopping black ears,
and neck. . . . She worked
until the steaming length of him
rushed out onto the ground, then
turned and licked him with her wide
pink tongue. He lifted up his head
and looked around.

The herd pressed close to see, then
frolicked up the bank, flicking
their tails. It looked like revelry.
The farmer set off for the barn,
swinging in a widening arc
a frayed and knotted scrap of rope.

Baobab Fruit Picking
(or Development in Monkey Bay)

for Mary and David Kerr

JACK MAPANJE *South Africa*

"We've fought before, but this is worse than rape!"
In the semi-Sahara October haze, the raw jokes

Of Balamanja women are remarkable. The vision
We revel in has sent their husbands to the mines

Of Jo'burg, to buy us large farms, she insists.
But here, the wives survive by their wits & sweat:

Shoving dead cassava stalks into rocks, catching
Fish in tired chitenje cloths with kids, picking   .

Baobab fruit & whoring. The bark from the baobab
They strip into strings for their reed wattle,

The fruit they crack, scoop out the white, mix with
Goat milk, "there's porridge for today, children!"

The shell is drinking gourd or firewood split
(They used to grate the hard cores into girls'

Initiation oil once). "But you imported the Boers,
Who visited our Chief at dawn, promising boreholes!"

These pine cottages on the beach shot up instead, some
With barbed wire fences fifty yards into the lake!

(What cheek!) Now each weekend, the "blighted-tomato-
thighs in reeking loin-cloths" come, boating, grinning

At them baobab fruit picking. "My house was right
Here!" Whoever dares check these Balamanja dreamers?

IV

The Removal of Our Village

The Woodcut on the Cover of
Robert Frost's *Complete Poems*

for Wendell Berry

HAYDEN CARRUTH *United States*

A man plowing starts at the side of the field
Nearer home and works outward and away.
Why? Because plowing is always an adventure.
Then walking home with the horses at end of day.

Afraid of the Countryside

SAKUTARO HAGIWARA *Japan*

I'm afraid of the countryside,
afraid of rows of long slender rice stalks
trembling in deserted paddies of the countryside.
Afraid of swarms of poor human beings living in dark houses.

When I sit on a ridge between paddies,
the billow-like weight of the soil darkens my heart,
the rotten smell of the soil blackens my skin,
the winter-barren lonely nature oppresses my life.

The air of the countryside is gloomy, heavy,
the touch of the countryside, gritty, sickening.
When I sometimes think of the countryside,
I'm tormented by the smell of rough animal skin.
I'm afraid of the countryside.
The countryside is a pale dream in a fever.

And You, Vanya . . .

YURY ODARCHENKO *Russia*

And you, Vanya,
Go and cut up that black rooster.
—What for?
The little rooster sings to us at dawn.
—It sure does.
But you must be alive to listen to it.
And to be alive,
You must eat.
Vanya cut up the rooster.
Now everybody's alive, sitting and listening
To the little hen cackling.
Crying for its rooster.

Translated by Nina Kossman

Pastoral

ANNIE DILLARD *United States*

Sometimes when a peasant moves with the plough and the oxen
Over the broad surface of the field,
It is as if the vault of the sky might take

Up into itself the peasant, the plough, and the oxen.
It is as though time had been sown into silence.
The eye of the gods falls on the figures and they

Increase. A bird flies slowly into the sky.
Its movements are trails that keep the silence enclosed.
Grain and stars shine through the mist and haze.

Animals lead silence through the world of man.
The cattle: the broad surface of their backs . . .
It is as if they were carrying silence.

Two cows in a field moving with a man beside them:
It is as if the man were pouring down silence
From the backs of the animals on to the fields.

The Funeral

NORMAN DUBIE *United States*

It felt like the zero in brook ice.
She was my youngest aunt, the summer before
We had stood naked
While she stiffened and giggled, letting the minnows
Nibble at her toes. I was almost four —
That evening she took me
To the springhouse where on the scoured planks
There were rows of butter in small bricks, a mold
Like ermine on the cheese,
And cut onions to rinse the air
Of the black, sickly-sweet meats of rotting pecans.

She said butter was colored with marigolds
Plucked down by the marsh
With its tall grass and miner's-candles.
We once carried the offal's pail beyond the barn
To where the fox could be caught in meditation.
Her bed linen smelled of camphor. We went

In late March for her burial. I heard the men talk.
I saw the minnows nibble at her toe.
And Uncle Peter, in a low voice, said
The cancer ate her like horse piss eats deep snow.

The Removal of Our Village, KwaBhanya

MBUYISENI MTSHALI *South Africa*

O, I remember you,
my tiny little village of KwaBhanya
where my umbilical cord was cut with a reed knife;
where I yelled a scream of horror at being brought into this world,
where I inhaled the herbs burnt to banish the evil spirits,
that choked every infant born to the black mothers,
where my forefathers and my parents were masters of their lives,
and owners of their plots,
where they lived without paying any rent to Mlungu,
where we tilled the ground,
harvested a bountiful crop,
fresh mielie corn, large pumpkins
which we squashed into pulp
to make pumpkin broth and melon porridge;
and ate juicy calabashes, luscious peaches, plums and pears.

Mlungu came from the town of Vryheid (Freedom)
to deprive us of our liberty by his endless decrees
and pompous proclamations,
"All Bantu people of this slum and black spot must move."

We went on milking our cows,
Heleyisi and Batata.
I drank milk straight from the cow's udder
by squeezing the teats into my mouth;
we ladled rich cream in our claypots
and mixed the sour milk
together with fresh corn bread;
we stuffed ourselves full like piglets.

It was a blissful life.

It was an existence we savoured more than
Christians hanker for their Jesu and Heaven in the clouds;

we had our feet in the soil of our ancestors,
and we salted the soil with our tears during the drought,
and watered the crops with our sweat.

Alas, the sunshine of our happiness was short-lived;
dark clouds marched across the sky carrying guns,
and took up menacing positions above our heads.

And when I think of my boyhood
I feel I am bashing my head against a rock.
The rock is stone deaf to my cries;
I wish I could pinch it once
and make it wince with pain.

I see myself in short pants and khaki shirt,
running a race with my shadow,
trying to catch the tail of Gugu, our fluffy cat;
and then collide with my many friends —
Sikobho, Fabiyana, Thami, Jimisoni;
they are all dead now.
I will follow them
when crabs and frogs have grown horns.

I feel a million arrows pass through my heart,
my eyes turn into a stream of salty water,
I page through the flimsy salinity,
I see the broken graves of my grandfather and grandmother.

I hear their voices calling,
"Buya, light the lantern,
the stars are hidden in the sea cave,
the rain has gone to fetch them,
the sea is sorry it lashed the earth with thunderclaps."

I grope in the dark in the feeble light of my lantern,
the grave is ablaze,
the tombstones are smiling ghosts,
they are singing to me a valedictory hymn!

"Hhayi usizi lomunti omnyama e-Afrika . . .
O, the black man's sorrow in Africa."

I know the time is near,
Mlungu is coming to our village,
KwaBhanya will soon be dead;
the voices from the ghostly graves are warning me
to tell the villagers;
I dare not.

Then it was morning again,
as all mornings come in the morning
never at noon nor in the evening nor at night.
The morning brings the word from Pretoria,
as words come from Pretoria,
because only Pretoria has a mouth;
Cape Town has the brain to think
what the mouth has to say.
Only Johannesburg has the heart;
they say it has a heart of gold, maybe for whites,
and a clay heart for us blacks,
and of course Durban has a banana heart.

And the word was this . . .
"Bantu people of Bestersspruit, you must move . . . Julle moet
    trek."

Villagers gathered in clusters,
they called meeting after meeting,
and decided in unison to defy the word from Pretoria;
"Mlungu is mad, his head is full of shit, asihambi."

Then it was Monday morning,
as Monday mornings are ominous everywhere,
when army trucks trundled to a stop,
raising an acrid dust and petrol fumes
that filled our eyes with tears
and our mouths with unvomited puke.

Police in battle dress jumped out from the trucks,
they were armed to the teeth,
and as grim-faced as the white man
who hangs people in Pretoria.

"We told you to move . . . so trek nou."

We pleaded for an extension of time.

We wanted to harvest our crop,
we wanted to transfer our children to other schools,
we waited for the return of our husbands
and sons from the mines in Johannesburg.

We were taken by force
and put in row upon row of tents,
like prisoners of war in a camp,
while bulldozers razed our houses to the ground.

"Mlungu, how can you do this to us?
Look at what Mlungu the Christian is doing to us;
Mlungu, wait for our days of vengeance,
Mlungu, we are Zulus, born fighters,
we will take our spears and fight for our lands."

Mississippi Mysteries, Continued

AL YOUNG *United States*

Papa wasn't no fool, but neither was that farm.
You could stand nights on the front or back porch
and look clean into Heaven. Papa knew this.
Mama knew it, all the kids, the mules, cows,
chickens, goats, and all the cornstalks knew it.
Oh, God, why do you go around and around inventing
these worlds where birth must come to death,
where silence and slow time saw through all
feelings, all gravied thoughts; the bridges
we must cross but can't build on? If a tropical,
melony breeze came whooshing across the briarpatch
and tickled me sadly, it was because we were in July,
that hellacious month of jubilant weather nights.

The Planting of the Blue Corn

EDGAR GABRIEL SILEX *United States*

after the fields are planted
and the blue corn seeds are nestled
in the red earth   after the Corn Planter
has put away his sacred planting stick
he says a prayer to the quiet air
that hovers above the lines
marking the seeded fields

and then the wind puts on
its dancing moccasins and begins
to swirl   to spin above
the cleared and pregnant naked land
brushing up the red dust
from its grounded desert feet

and together they begin a choreographed
whirling and swinging
like little tornados pirouetting
together they marionette above
the corn rows   and the clouds

wishing not to be left out
begin to clap in rhythm
to the thrum of the rustling
sage leaves   and everyone
starts dancing in the dust of happiness

the mountains and the trees rattle
with the increasing crescendo
of the clapping clouds and the tumbleweeds
start rolling in a joyous laughter
and the clouds   too   begin to laugh
until their joyous tears fall
sending everyone scurrying away

from the planting festival below
and the dust lies back down
and the wind blows away
in search of other pregnant fields
and the rain falls
and the blue corn shoots
begin to grow

The Green Combine

JANET KAUFFMAN *United States*

When you drive by in your green combine
on its toy wheels and lifted V
cornhead, I hear you turn
at the driveway, slow like a plane gearing down,
the engines dying, coasting
until you're stopped at the porch.

And there you are with your headphones around your neck,
in the living room just like a brother
lost for years in abandoned mines
in Idaho, smiling
I came back.

We talk prices per bushel
and futures, the inexhaustible
statistics like kisses,
codes of the hybrids, Pioneer 412 C,
X-249, and the yields.

Outside the combine catches the rain; its bin fills.
The cab like a sacred place thrums with birds.
The green
rusts although vines from the side of the house
find their way there and wreathe
the choppers, the lengths of rollered belts,
battery, gears, the heart.

In your fields the corn lies down.
Deer, the escaped steers and cows
come there to feed.

What next? say the neighbors. They leap the porch railing,
to talk of neglect
and the things around here gone wild,
gone to seed.

Platt River Holdout

KATY PEAKE *United States*

Where last month tasseled ranks of corn linked
farm to farm across the prairie miles,
now each is solitaire, an island of abandoned totems,
squatting in the grit and silt of river leavings.

Here rib-sprung silos totter, stinking of fermented grain
in clouds of drunk and dying flies, above the sagging
roofs of barns and sheds where discs and harrows rust with
algae in their teeth and cows drowned in their stanchions.

Here hot winds fret the buried fields and pock the panes
of empty drift-flanked houses, spraddled derelict over
vine-stripped porches, like mired beasts listening
to the ceaseless night bird cries of dry windmills.

Here too a man plows, inscribing the legend of fifty years'
domain, the unmarked boundaries of his lost holdings so
fixed, he does not pause to note the turns or shift his head
to watch the crumbling furrows fill with dust behind him.

Once We Were Farmers

ELSA REDIVA E'DER *United States*

Once we were farmers
and we measured time
in distant moments
of new life

and our hopes dwelled
welled up through sweat and skin
unspoken and sacred

and on the rocks we let lie in the fields
we stenciled language
and fed the rainfall upon our stories
and moments circled above the earth

    till now

    unspoken is our passion
    our passion is the moon
    lying down
    in these moments
    in the fields O pen ing
    and in the rhythms of stillness
    we were life anew

we were farmers and midwives
and blood spilled towards the future
in rituals of ancient powers

we leaned toward the cries
of children who gave sound
to rocks we let lie in the fields

We sing
we sing with eloquent hunger.

Everything Else You Can Get You Take

ROBERT DANA *United States*

It's that kind of day.
Hay and panic grass
combed into rolling windrows.
Minstrel-faced sheep. A few
head of crossbred Charlies.

No place we ever imagined
we'd be. No sea's edge
where a low wave sputters,
ignites like a fuse, and races
hissing along the shore.
No thin, viral mist fizzing
the windshield, gorges rising
grey as China in the rain.

Only this long roll of
space where day lilies
leap any breaks in the fences,
flooding down ditches, orange
against the many colors of green —
only the jingle and ring of
morning crickets in the dew.

Don't ask how long we've
been here, or why we stayed.
You fall in love with
a climate. Everything else
you can get you take.

The Cucumber

to Ekber Babayev

NAZIM HIKMET *Germany*

The snow is knee-deep in the courtyard
and still coming down hard:
it hasn't let up all morning.
We're in the kitchen.
On the table, on the oilcloth, spring —
on the table there's a very tender young cucumber,
                        pebbly and fresh as a daisy.
We sit around the table staring at it.
It softly lights up our faces
and the very air smells fresh.
We sit around the table staring at it
— amazed,
            thoughtful,
                        optimistic —
as if in a dream.
On the table, on the oilcloth, hope —
on the table, beautiful days,
a cloud seeded with a green sun,
an emerald crowd impatient and on its way,
loves blooming openly —
on the table, there on the oilcloth, a very tender young
                                    cucumber,
                  pebbly and fresh as a daisy.
The snow is knee-deep in the courtyard
and coming down hard.
It hasn't let up all morning.

March 1960, Moscow

Translated by Randy Blasing and Mutlu Konuk

Green Fields

W. S. MERWIN *United States*

By this part of the century few are left who believe
    in the animals for they are not there in the carved parts
of them served on plates and the pleas from the slatted trucks
    are sounds of shadows that possess no future
there is still game for the pleasure of killing
    and there are pets for the children but the lives that followed
courses of their own other than ours and older
    have been migrating before us some are already
far on the way and yet Peter with his gaunt cheeks
    and point of white beard the face of an aged Lawrence
Peter who had lived on from another time and country
    and who had seen so many things set out and vanish
still believed in heaven and said he had never once
    doubted it since his childhood on the farm in the days
of the horses he had not doubted it in the worst
    times of the Great War and afterward and he had come
to what he took to be a kind of earthly
    model of it as he wandered south in his sixties
by that time speaking the language well enough
    for them to make him out he took the smallest roads
into a world he thought was a thing of the past
    with wildflowers he scarcely remembered and neighbors
working together scything the morning meadows
    turning the hay before the noon meal bringing it in
by milking time husbandry and abundance
    all the virtues he admired and their reward bounteous
in the eyes of a foreigner and there he remained
    for the rest of his days seeing what he wanted to see
until the winter when he could no longer fork
    the earth in his garden and then he gave away
his house land everything and committed himself
    to a home to die in an old chateau where he lingered
for some time surrounded by those who had lost
    the use of body or mind and as he lay there he told me
that the wall by his bed opened almost every day

and he saw what was really there and it was eternal life
as he recognized at once when he saw the gardens
he had made and the green fields where he had been
a child and his mother was standing there then the wall would close
and around him again were the last days of the world

Cabbages at Night

HASEGAWA RYUSEI *Japan*

On the thick concrete floor
of the deserted vegetable market
empty into the night,
seven or eight piles of winter cabbages
are left.

Emitting a blue glow,
they light up
every corner of the high ceiling
supported by its tall pillars.

Now a wholesaler
with the collar of his jumper turned up
comes swiftly
into the market like a shadow.
Two unseasonable green caterpillars
that have been crawling
over the mountain of cabbages
suddenly stop moving
as if they were dead.

It is dark outside.
The cold wind that will blow until morning
passes
through thin icicles.

Translated by Naoshi Koriyama and Edward Lueders

The Hen

MARVIN BELL *United States*

hungers to whistle. She longs to hear a cry ring out
from all the bottled-up mothers. At dawn
in the barnyard, see her throat squeeze
from the effort, and her clumpy body go up on tiptoe
to reach a higher register. Hear the gravel rattle
in her craw as she croaks her egg song.
She is the ballerina of ballerinas, the queen
of torch, the damsel in distress sure to be saved
for her great beauty, her way with music
and the frilly glow of freedom in her feathers.

The rooster, on flat feet. He feels like a policeman
inside a whistle, seeing the robbers
make off with the loot. While she feels like a wife in port
watching for a ship in a bottle. O anger suffused
by clucking and scratching, oh hunger that rings, dashing
itself on the stones of a common indigestion —
or else she will be asked to walk a line in the dirt
so that she might be hypnotized for the ax!
The hen knows hunger is a bag of bones. She has
a straw mattress and an underestimated egg.

The Memory

MAYA ANGELOU *United States*

Cotton rows crisscross the world
   And dead-tired nights of yearning
Thunderbolts on leather strops
   And all my body burning

Sugar cane reach up to God
   And every baby crying
Shame the blanket of my night
   And all my days are dying

Some Grass along a Ditch Bank

LARRY LEVIS *United States*

I don't know what happens to grass.
But it doesn't die, exactly.
It turns white, in winter, but stays there,
A few yards from the ditch,
Then comes back in March,
Turning a green that has nothing
To do with us.
Mostly, it's just yellow, or tan.
It blends in,
Swayed by the wind, maybe, but not by any emotion,
Or partisan stripe.
You can misread it, at times:
I have seen it almost appear
To fight long & well
For its right to be, & be grass, when
I tried pulling it out.
I thought I could almost sense it digging in,
Not with reproach, exactly,
But with a kind of rare tact that I miss,
Sometimes, in others.
And besides, if you really wanted it out,
You'd have to disc it under,
Standing on a shuddering Case tractor,
And staring into the distance like
Somebody with a vision
In the wrong place for visions.
With time, you'd feel silly.
And, always, it comes back:
At the end of some winter when
The sky has neither sun, nor snow,
Nor anything personal,
You'd be wary of any impulse
That seemed mostly cosmetic.
It's all a matter of taste,
And how taste changes.

Besides, in March, the fields are wet;
The trucks & machinery won't start,
And the blades of the disc won't turn,
Usually, because of the rust.
That's when you notice the grass coming back,
In some other spot, & with a different look
This time, as if it had an idea
For a peninsula, maybe, or its shape
Reclining on a map you almost
Begin to remember.
In March, my father spent hours
Just piecing together some puzzle
That might start up a tractor,
Or set the tines of a cultivator
Or spring tooth right,
And do it without paying money.
Those rows of gray earth that look "combed,"
Between each row of vines,
And run off to the horizon
As you drive past?
You could almost say
It was almost pretty.
But this place isn't France.
For years, they've made only raisins,
And a cheap, sweet wine.
And someone had to work late,
As bored as you are, probably,
But with the added headache of
Owning some piece of land
That never gave up much
Without a mute argument.
The lucky sold out to subdividers,
But this is for one who stayed,
And how, after a few years,
He even felt sympathy for grass —
Then felt *that* turn into a resentment
Which grew, finally, into
A variety of puzzled envy:
Turning a little grass under

With each acre,
And turning it under for miles,
While half his life, spent
On top of a tractor,
Went by, unnoticed, without feast days
Or celebrations — opening his mailbox
At the roadside which was incapable
Of looking any different —
More picturesque, or less common —
The rank but still blossoming weeds
Stirring a little, maybe,
As you drove past,
But then growing still again.

V

Twenty Horses Wild

The Quality of Sprawl

LES MURRAY *Australia*

Sprawl is the quality
of the man who cut down his Rolls-Royce
into a farm utility truck, and sprawl
is what the company lacked when it made repeated efforts
to buy the vehicle back and repair its image.

Sprawl is doing your farming by aeroplane, roughly,
or driving a hitchhiker that extra hundred miles home.
It is the rococo of being your own still centre.
It is never lighting cigars with ten-dollar notes:
that's idiot ostentation and murder of starving people.
Nor can it be bought with the ash of million-dollar deeds.

Sprawl lengthens the legs; it trains greyhounds on liver and beer.
Sprawl almost never says Why not? with palms comically raised
nor can it be dressed for, not even in running shoes worn
with mink and a nose ring. That is Society. That's Style.
Sprawl is more like the thirteenth banana in a dozen
or anyway the fourteenth.

Sprawl is Hank Stamper in *Never Give an Inch*
bisecting an obstructive official's desk with a chainsaw.
Not harming the official. Sprawl is never brutal
though it's often intransigent. Sprawl is never Simon de Montfort
at a town-storming: Kill them all! God will know his own.
Knowing the man's name this was said to might be sprawl.

Sprawl occurs in art. The fifteenth to twenty-first
lines in a sonnet, for example. And in certain paintings;
I have sprawl enough to have forgotten which paintings.
Turner's glorious *Burning of the Houses of Parliament*
comes to mind, a doubling bannered triumph of sprawl —
except, he didn't fire them.

Sprawl gets up the nose of many kinds of people
(every kind that comes in kinds) whose futures don't include it.
Some decry it as criminal presumption, silken-robed Pope
    Alexander
dividing the new world between Spain and Portugal.
If he smiled *in petto* afterwards, perhaps the thing did have sprawl.

Sprawl is really classless, though. It's John Christopher Frederick
    Murray
asleep in his neighbours' best bed in spurs and oilskins
but not having thrown up:
sprawl is never Calum who, drunk, along the hallways of our
    house,
reinvented the Festoon. Rather
it's Beatrice Miles going twelve hundred ditto in a taxi,
No Lewd Advances, No Hitting Animals, No Speeding,
on the proceeds of her two-bob-a-sonnet Shakespeare readings.
An image of my country. And would that it were more so.

No, sprawl is full-gloss murals on a council-house wall.
Sprawl leans on things. It is loose-limbed in its mind.
Reprimanded and dismissed
it listens with a grin and one boot up on the rail
of possibility. It may have to leave the Earth.
Being roughly Christian, it scratches the other cheek
and thinks it unlikely. Though people have been shot for sprawl.

Agriculture

for Richard Borgmann

JAMES GALVIN *United States*

Tonight the rain can't stand up straight, but once,
Watching over my shoulder the ten wheeling suns
Of the double siderake rolling newmown hay
Over and over and over and over
Into the windrow like a thick green rope,
I was nothing
But a window sailing through the night,
And once when twenty horses wild together
All winter, galloped towards me down the road
With Harrison whooping behind them and
The little stock dog barking at their heels,
And me there to turn them into the corral
From the middle of the road, their eighty
Hooves a roll of thunder in the earth,
Me with a stupid piece of rope in my hand,
I was nothing
But a window sailing through the night.

Carbuncle

MURIEL ZELLER *United States*

she saw the earth redd
center of the sore
in day's last light,
wondered how long
since the carbuncle broke,
its dried export darkened
by dirt and debris. she approached
the mare cautiously, field bred
she was somewhat wild,
wore no leather. bribed with molasses-laced grain
she gave in to the halter.
confined to the barn

their tenebrous shapes
blended to the walls
enclosing manger, stanchions, hay storage,
feed ricks for orphaned calves.
outside dusk held
the receding engine sound:
truck falling into ruts
gunning over rocks
on its way to fetch
the veterinarian. she
fingered the perimeter
of erupted flesh,
murmured into the black neck,
stroked coat growing blacker.
movement remains:

the mare's impatient head shake,
the constant push against night
from her nostrils,
floating dust,
mice marking
a trail over the mouldering hay-dirt floor,

cooling redwood
shrinking to its nails.
she cooed

and cooed like pigeons that roosted before owls who watched
and kept the mice numbered.

Buck

PAUL ZARZYSKI *United States*

The December my horse died, I did not
go to midnight mass
to celebrate with a single sip of wine
Christ's birth. Instead, lit
between a nimbus moon and new snow,
I guzzled mezcal and mimicked the caroling
coyotes down the crick
where weeks earlier I dragged Buck
behind the pickup — horizontal
hooves at an awkward trot
in the side mirror, an image
I'll take with me to hell. No backhoe,
no D-8 Cat to dig a grave with, I left
him in deep bunchgrass, saffron
belly toward the south
like a warm porch light thrown
suddenly over those singing
No-el, No-el. . . .
　　　　　　　　Riding the same ground
that past spring for horned cow skulls
to adorn our gates, I spotted four
bleached white as puffballs,
methodically stuffed them
into a *never-tear* trash bag,
balanced the booty
off one thigh and tried to hold
jog-trot Buck to a walk,
my forefinger hefting
the left rein to curb
his starboard glance.
　　　　　　　　One by one,
like spook-show aliens hatching
from human brisket, white shoots popped
through that hot black plastic
gleaming in noon sun that turned

132

my grasp to butterfat. And when I reached,
lifting to retwist my grip,
it was sputnik flying low, it was
Satan's own crustacean unleashed, it was THE
prehistoric, eight-horned horse-eating bug
that caught Buck's eye
the instant his lit fuse hit powder. Lord,
how that old fat pony, living
up to his name one last time,
flashed his navel at angels,
rattled and rolled my skulls like dice,
and left me on all fours,
as he did that Christmas — high —
lonesomed, hurt, and howling
not one holy word toward the bones.

Horse-doctor

KATHERINE PIERPOINT *Great Britain*

Little old man with a strong farmyard smell on him
Of mud and damp rubber and root vegetables
Totters into this yard, bandy as a baby,
And can tell straight off what's wrong with a pony
Just from being quiet in the stable with it a while.
Sees things in the way they use their eyes,
Gets ideas or hunches suddenly, same as they do;
Or standing in the paddock, watches which herbs they pull
From far back in the hedgerow.
Sees which way their need will drive them.

Can tell if there's a speck of mould in the hay.
Gets out an old curry-comb with half the teeth gone,
Then runs it through the coat and smells
With his head down and mouth open at it like a dog.
He drenches a sick one using an old horn,
And a blue glass bottle with a crusty cork.
They'll take it. They'll be kicking the place down,
Flaring, all teeth and eyes and flattened ears,
Then go all quiet under his hands,
While we can't get behind them, can't get near them.

The dogs love him. He brings a bag of bits for them;
Best of all when he's seen the blacksmith for the parings.
Throws them crescent moons of hoofcuts —
A rind still burnt and smoky
That goes pattering down on the stones — the dogs rushing for
    them.
Could be anything in that blue glass bottle,
But the old feller knows his stuff all right.
He'll part a pile of droppings with his boot and
Show you the story in it — can tell the weather from it —
Like those Eskimos with all their snow,
Twenty different kinds of shit, at least.

Egg and Daughter Night, April 1951
WILLIAM MATTHEWS *United States*

So much of the soil out here has been sown by wind
that the rolls and dune-like tilts of the mild hills
under snow seem to go on forever, like winter itself.

And in early spring: waves and waves of beige stubble.
The longer disuse reigns, the more its subjects look alike.
But now we're in the fields. See that flash of alfalfa

two roads over? The loneliness of farming is finally
communal: from Nebraska to Ohio all the soil
not paved or built on gets turned once a year.

On egg and daughter night Mary Beth and Sue
sit so stiff on the truck they could have been ironed.
We'll sell some eggs and buy some hail insurance,

a few racks of pool, fifty lbs. of flour, coffee
in three-lb. cans. Wind is the other half of family life.
The wind unwinds in the truck-thick streets.

Spring/Summer 1986

Appetite

MAXINE KUMIN *United States*

I eat these
wild red raspberries
still warm from the sun
and smelling faintly of jewelweed
in memory of my father

tucking the napkin
under his chin and bending
over an ironstone bowl
of the bright drupelets
awash in cream

my father
with the sigh of a man
who has seen all and been redeemed
said time after time
as he lifted his spoon

men kill for this.

Untitled

TOMAZ SALAMUN *Yugoslavia*

if you grab a chicken by its feet
and by its wings and with sudden movement
turn it on its back and at the same time
slowly press it against the table
it will stiffen in that unnatural position
drift into sleep its feet stretched out
without strength its talons trembling
occasionally and the chicken staying like that
as if tied to the table even if you were
to step aside imperceptibly the chicken
will remain ten or more minutes as if
spellbound

The Bogie-Wife

KATHLEEN JAMIE *Scotland*

She hoists her thigh over back fences,
not down the street, her feet squash
worms, hands stained brown as dung.

She flusters hens, looking for babies:
one eye swiveling in the middle of her forehead.
She leaves, like a yeti
the proof of her footprint.

Traffic on the road ignores her
the daylight is both broad and long;
our nouveau arrivistes; businessmen, journalists,
know her for a daft village story, like the Black Beast.

She's simple, gets tangled in the netting
of raspberry-groves; but canny: keeps
to the railway wall, compost heaps.

She can smell babies, will push
between laundry hung to dry
arms, strong as plum-boughs
twisting into fruit.

It's just her nature, she means no harm
but the old wives run her out of town,
some banging pot-lids as others shout
This is Private Property! Ye've nae right!

But she is charming when cornered,
speaks a nice Scots,
wears a fresh tee-shirt and attractive batik trousers.

The Barn-yard

SHEILA CUSSONS *South Africa*

The pigsty did not reek:
it smelled pleasantly crass-sour-rotten,
and the gluttonous snouts in hogwash and gourd
and the unmentionable mud was the most wonderful
most daring bad manners imaginable —
I loved the pigsty far removed
at the lower end of the barn-yard,
behind a row of cypresses, and liked to sit on its wall
and sniff in deeply the feral scent
and be amazed at animals so shamelessly
gluttonous they even guzzle with their snouts;
and their ugly heavy mugs with the stupid
white-lashed eyelets like something from Grimm
or Andersen. Indeed, the pigs were Somebodies,
like princes disguised by withered old witches
or Circe's swine-sailors —
Nearly sun-blind I dreamt about them,
until mud-mellow, so strong and richly-sweet
saturated my young veins, the magical enchantment
of all the summers of my youth —
Back in the house:
Good Lord one really can't bear this
Grandmother piously complained of the heat
and, hell but it's hot, bluntly
from my slightly more carnal mother:
how could they understand that the scorching day
and the pigsty
was a heaven to me, a fable unrivalled —
Also the lost paradise was just outside the house:
a big old plum-tree with sinful fruit
which fell from above just like us,
and if you picked one up you could still see in time
how the evil quickly recoiled
back into the injured flesh —
O lost barn-yard, in you I could find the whole Old Testament
and the Greek legends and Andersen.

Translated by Johann de Lange

Flirting with a Pig

ALEKSANDAR RISTOVIC *Serbia*

Come to me pig, you who dress yourself as a courtier
    while still wallowing in the mud,
come to me with your small eyes averted.
I have understanding for your embarrassment
    and for your vanity.

It's not right for a poet to like the same things
    you do,
but there's something dear to me in your debauchery,
to which you yield with permanent ambivalence.

Still, the devil waits for you in the slaughterhouse.
He has fat fingers, a sheepskin coat, and fine
    cutting instruments.
He stands with legs spread apart in the middle of a large room,
    wearing rubber boots and playing with knives.

In the meantime, his helper rinses the wooden pail
    and watches the boss's daughter climb down the ladder,
lifting her skirt so that her pink soles and shins show.

Come to me, pig, mistress of the bog,
I'd like to whisper sweet nothings into your wide ear
    before they lead you away,
by turns throwing curses and praises upon you.

Translated by Charles Simic

A Land of Drought

MAXAMED CABDILLE XASAN *Somalia*

All these were mine —
Camels newly-calved, cattle plump of flesh,
A stock of sheep and goats,
Skimmed milk enough to plunge my mouth in deep and gulp it
    down,
An abundance of wealth,
And ghee churned in a great jar made of camelskin.
I had the meat of a gelded camel to eat,
Red meat and white and pieces of fat,
And the recesses of my hut were filled with silk and fine cloth.
Those were prosperous days when I stayed in the hills of Ayl!

It was not my idea that I should move away from there
And troubles broke upon me
As soon as my camels were loaded for the journey.
Men who did not know the will of the Lord
Poured away the contentment I had enjoyed —
It was they who forced me to come to the Nugaal
For I myself received no inner guidance in the matter.
I was not pleased with the plan, but they drove me onwards —
Why else would I have moved my household
From its dwelling-place there on the hill?

As I set down my family on this plain of Doodi
I saw that even a goat would go hungry here.
The herds were undone to find themselves amidst this bitter scrub
And the strongest of camels have weakened for lack of sustenance.

I uprooted myself from a place where rich grass grew for me.
In those days there was lush growth wherever I turned my face —
In those days a *jeerin* fruit, big as a man's head,
Would be put to cook in heated sand for me —

In those days I needed to assign for grazing
A mere quarter of the grass that was newly springing.

Had I but stayed in the Hawd
I would not now be afflicted by grinding want.
And yet how warmly they recommended this forsaken region,
Where the ranging beasts of prey pace swiftly round me
And where if a rotting carcass meets my sight
It proves to be that of a man or a woman or a child.

This is a place without one patch of ground
Where the wild game herds could graze,
It is a place where beasts must pluck
Small mouthfuls here and there of scrub and straw,
It is a place of no abiding use,
A place where teeth will find no food to chew!

Translated by B. W. Andrzejewski and Sheila Andrzejewski

The Bitch

SERGEY YESENIN *Russia*

In the morning the bitch whelped
Seven reddish-brown pups,
In the rye barn where a row
Of bast mats gleamed like gold.

She fondled them till evening,
Licking their pelts smooth,
And underneath her, the snow
Melted out in the heat.

But at dusk, when the hens
Were roosting on the perch,
There came the grim-faced master
Who stuffed the pups in a sack.

The bitch bounded alongside him,
Over the snow-deep fields,
And the icy surface of the water
Shuddered a long, long while.

And when at last she struggled home,
Licking the sweat from her sides,
To her the moon above the house
Seemed like one of the pups.

Whimpering loudly she gazed up
Limpidly into the dark,
While over the hill, the slender moon
Slid into the fields beyond.

And softly, as when someone,
Jesting, throws her a stone,
Her tears, like golden stars,
Trickled down into the snow.

Translated by Daniel Weissbort

A Young Land Cultivation Department Technician's Recitative on Irises

KENJI MIYAZAWA *Japan*

Again separating myself
from the surveying group
I have come back over the beautiful green highlands
visiting on the way
innumerable dense, sensuous clusters of purple,
gatherings of irises fragrant in the sun.
To carry around pointed transits and striped poles
trying to compete with ancient Kitagami for age,
to cut railway and paddies and chip rocks
from a section of the semi-plain
that has stored days since the Cretaceous period
only to turn out two maps —
that, under the azure vault,
is unequivocally the Original Sin.
Tomorrow, quivering motors
and huge plows shining dull
will bury under countless rows of overturned black earth
hundreds of these tall pliant flower stalks
and each one of these petals and pistils
that look like silk or blue wax.
Then they will become dreary humus
and help grow coarse tough corn and ears of oat,
but I, along with this clear south wind,
cannot but give the flowers
all my helpless caresses and boundless love.

Translated by Hiroaki Sato

The Biting Insects

GALWAY KINNELL *United States*

The biting insects don't like the blood of people who dread dying.

They prefer the blood of people who can imagine themselves
entering other life-forms.

These are the ones the mosquito sings to in the dark and the deer
fly orbits and studies with yellow eyes.

In the other animals the desire to die comes when existing wears
out existence.

In us this desire can come too early, and we kill ourselves, or it may
never come, and we have to be dragged away.

Not many are able to die well, not even Jesus going back to his
father.

And yet dying gets done — and Eddie Jewell coming up the road
with his tractor on a gooseneck trailer and seeing an owl lifting
its wings as it alights on the ridgepole of this red house, Galway,
will know that now it is you being accepted back into the family
of mortals.

Washing the Grain

YASMINE GOONERATNE *Australia*

Round and round the year tilts
from night-time to dawn from sunlight to shadow
and the pale days falling from this side to that
yield a fine cloudiness only

We are so far now, so far, cry the grains
the home-field only a memory warm
in the husk
and that too sloughed off
that too lost
in the mortar's pounding

Round and round spin the days
another year of this churning
and tilting, washing at last
quite over the rim
will we lie in clear water
pure, transparent,
delicately separate?

We shall become
consumable! our pale substance
will satisfy somebody

and this dark grit
trapped in the bowl's fine furrows
may be disposed of, thrown
out upon the wattles and dry grass

Farm Wife

ELLEN BRYANT VOIGT *United States*

Dark as the spring river, the earth
opens each damp row as the farmer
swings the far side of the field.
The blackbirds flash their red
wing patches and wheel in his wake,
down to the black dirt; the windmill
grinds in its chain rig and tower.

In the kitchen, his wife is baking.
She stands in the door in her long white
gloves of flour. She cocks her head and
tries to remember, turns like the moon
toward the sea-black field. Her belly
is rising, her apron fills like a sail.
She is gliding now, the windmill churns
beneath her, she passes the farmer,
the fine map of the furrows.
The neighbors point to the bone-white
spot in the sky.
                    Let her float
like a fat gull that swoops and circles,
before her husband comes in for supper,
before her children grow up and leave her,
before the pulley cranks her down
the dark shaft, and the church blesses
her stone bed, and the earth seals
its black mouth like a scar.

Bread and Wine

NINA CASSIAN *Romania*

We said there'd be a celebration . . .
There wasn't.
And so I dressed for no apparent
reason in the height of fashion.

I waited for you till dawn.
All night I waited.
In the carafe — stagnant wine,
on the tables — stale bread.

And when day came upon the land
— and I knew it would remain there —
I took the flowers from my hair
with a withered hand.

Translated by Brenda Walker and Andrea Deletant

delta farm

DENNIS SCHMITZ *United States*

a friend weighs little a wife
makes the body heavy
as she swims away in the marriage
sheets — she seems more
strange than my mother's

face surfacing
in memory. so the drowned
displace the living —
not my wife's but
mother's thirst dries the sweaty

fingerprints
from the handle of the short hoe
or cutter
bar skimming the overflow
our salty bodies deposit between
windrows. together we pressed

drool from the sugar
beets & threw
or wished to throw our bodies
like pulp to the few
hogs we kept for meat on the tufted
mud of an upstream
island. this is the sweetness we refused
one another.

this neighbor is married
to solitude
another whose bridal sheets still smell
fresh drinks
greenish mouthsful from the cistern
children won't grow

up their roots churn in
the cultivated
zones fractured by a hundred
canal reflections.

when women visit
they only fix cots in fallen
down coolie shacks below
the town produce
sheds now abandoned & shifting
with the sun's weight.
when they leave boys

will lie restlessly
fishing in the narrow
beds skiffs make, between the pilings
hear the sheet
metal pop nails to trail
in a swifter river.
late November: a sixty-knot
squall through

the Straits breaks
levees, backs salt water miles
inland to preserve
what it kills. animal features
wake on the bedroom windows —
buck deer the flood divorced;
our cow sewn with scars
bawls, against the dawn rubs
her painful ballast

of milk. my wife by instinct
washes her own
breasts before our daughter
feeds. birds in refugee dozens
scatter as I walk
a smaller yard. for days only boats

define the horizon. only the doctor
salt-stained
like us in boots & overalls
scares us. our daughter crawls
through fever one week
then her mother the week after
dies. my wife,
still my wife, what I have
of you, this residue, this love-

salt, will not let me cross private
places in my body
anymore. without you
I can only continue a snail inside
my shell of sleep trailing sticky
dreams. nowhere to walk I go
away from you.

I am forty-two, my body
twenty-five.
my skin recopies over
& over my small daughter's

hand barely
holding against its current.
once I wanted to be still
water, a puddle the sky
fell in or halo
my forehead molds from the saturated
marsh when I bend

my face to the first
unconfirmed rice shoot.
now I wait for the March-fed
river to clean
the delta, knead our thought-
out acres of orchard high
ground where picking ladders descend

legless into their own
reflections. the bottomland rice
is lost but these trees
reach deeper. rings of salt show
each step back the sea
takes. swaying from tree
to tree at last my daughter learns

to walk.

Reading in Place

MARK STRAND *United States*

Imagine a poem that starts with a couple
Looking into a valley, seeing their house, the lawn
Out back with its wooden chairs, its shady patches of green,
Its wooden fence, and beyond the fence the rippled silver sheen
Of the local pond, its far side a tangle of sumac, crimson
In the fading light. Now imagine somebody reading the poem
And thinking, "I never guessed it would be like this,"
Then slipping it into the back of a book while the oblivious
Couple, feeling nothing is lost, not even the white
Streak of a flicker's tail that catches their eye, nor the slight
Toss of leaves in the wind, shift their gaze to the wooden dome
Of a nearby hill where the violet spread of dusk begins.
But the reader, out for a stroll in the autumn night, with all
The imprisoned sounds of nature dying around him, forgets
Not only the poem, but where he is, and thinks instead
Of a bleak Venetian mirror that hangs in a hall
By a curving stair, and how the stars in the sky's black glass
Sink down and the sea heaves them ashore like foam.
So much is adrift in the ever-opening rooms of elsewhere,
He cannot remember whose house it was, or when he was there.
Now imagine he sits years later under a lamp
And pulls a book from the shelf; the poem drops
To his lap. The couple are crossing a field
On their way home, still feeling that nothing is lost,
That they will continue to live harm-free; sealed
In the twilight's amber weather. But how will the reader know,
Especially now that he puts the poem, without looking,
Back in the book, the book where a poet stares at the sky
And says to a blank page, "Where, where in Heaven am I?"

In the Pasture

JORIE GRAHAM *United States*

What am I supposed to put now
into the sea of fulfillment, the broken record of swaying
                              plenitudes?
I press out hard
along the hurt — the campaign road — I press my thoughts, my
    tiny informers.
The earth curves more than I had thought
at first.
My mind, my thoughts in uniforms,
I press them out like little hieroglyphs onto the mudslide
where clods and lips are moving.
Who will you be?
What will you say when it says *repeat after me*
and you can't hear for the din
the black soil makes?
You come with your ploughshare, there, in your mouth —
it is sharp, it works for free which sharpens it, it cuts
into any distance freely thinking how good to die —
half out of their mind the words run fast and hard
over the muddy fields, seeking out woods and boundaries
— splendid declivities.
Who will you be when it comes your turn?
When I look up I see the body of my friend climb up
                         over the hilly rise
and redescend. There is an *other* side (my mind
knows this). I see my friend
climb down, straight down, into the open where there once
                        was pasture,
I see the sunlight beat him down,
I see how hard it beats with its clean sticks.
I see him going on in — it's *down* of course — under such
loving, into the mound it has
prepared for him, this golden freedom with its
                filamentary
sticks.

Later, at night, the fires on the horizon will make splendidly
clear who we are and who (I sleep so badly now)
they are. *You have to live* something keeps whispering, by day, in
sun, under its army's yellowest of boots . . .
And you: it is so prominent the way
                   you walk
over this soil, your soil, your mind held up there
in its fiery cavity — even the *day before*
               yesterday
still sparkling like oxygen in there — ah —
how much room you carry about in you over this field —
And tell me, did you volunteer?
Are you the last free man alive?
Are you *full of life* — billowing dresses on the lines,
blowsy hypotheses the butterflies can make over
                      their field
Can you pick your way among the
among? And the illustration of . . . ? And
the once-still architecture of
            the grandeur of
the sensible? the obvious? the inevitable? the true? —
the chestnut trees, the clean white napkins folded
                    under there?
the stars in the day-sky? —
the petticoat of morning-mist and the great-coat of
frost? What is it
my friend will have to find, breaking down and breaking down?
The earth curves more than we had imagined.
The slope cannot be staved against.
Rainwaters, the day-before-yesterday, the syllable
that grows its root into some tiny sleeping god
and makes that great sleep shudder-back
awake. The *last slaves*, when will they be alive?
The space in the heart, when will it be planted shut,
                    tamped-down,
choked-off with root, with growth,
with the simple obligation to blossom,
that final, thirstless, silencing.
My friend is lying in the earth. No, my love is

in the earth. He's weathering, gingerly, the hurt of its
                              downslope,
so that I can't see him anymore from here.
Materiality has dwindled.
What is it, muddy god, that has increased
                        therefore,
according to your law?
The day before the day before yesterday looks
spruced-up here in my cavity, my hole,
my grandest architecture of
syllabled — form building — sparkling clean — numb lidded
                                        gaze.
There's a book lying in the dust where we last lay.
The grass is bloody under it, but that's a
whim of blood, you know, a tiny thirst.
What does Paris look like now?
The eye darkens and the great cities kneel.
The monster of the mind moves easily among its marl,
its constant inward-sucking curl —
the day is measured-out in grams of light —
the monster, measured out in grams of light,
moves gently over the playing field,
dragon of changes and adjustments,
mightiness of redefining and refinement.
I love the uniforms my thoughts are wearing.
The heels, the sleeves. The black where nothing is wasted.
I love the stitchwork, each breath threading hard and tight
                              into each next breath,
holding the great-coat on
that we be better-looking,
elegant informers, so well-dressed as to almost be
                            transparent.
Tender, like the pasture.
Thick and clear, like a hole that can be jumped into — oh
earth, voice, string, gardener, lens.
Hear the hard damp in these our syllables.
We dare not pray. Hear us as the cloth
the needle.
The low buzz of the trees in inconstant wind

terrifies.
The leader here has cheeks shaved clean
and can't misfire
because he is enslaved and as god's son
is not allowed to miss.
Someone bites his cigarette.
Someone bites down hard and lets himself go
thinking how much he'd like to measure and to draw
this hole he's forced into,
how much he loves the soil they're shoving now
— lovers of poems, of flowerings, of all misdelivered messages —
down his wide throat.

The Simple Truth

PHILIP LEVINE *United States*

I bought a dollar and a half's worth of small red potatoes,
took them home, boiled them in their jackets
and ate them for dinner with a little butter and salt.
Then I walked through the dried fields
on the edge of town. In middle June the light
hung on in the dark furrows at my feet,
and in the mountain oaks overhead the birds
were gathering for the night, the jays and mockers
squawking back and forth, the finches still darting
into the dusty light. The woman who sold me
the potatoes was from Poland; she was someone
out of my childhood in a pink spangled sweater and sunglasses
praising the perfection of all her fruits and vegetables
at the road-side stand and urging me to taste
even the pale, raw sweet corn trucked all the way,
she swore, from New Jersey. "Eat, eat," she said,
"Even if you don't I'll say you did."
        Some things
you know all your life. They are so simple and true
they must be said without elegance, meter and rhyme,
they must be laid on the table beside the salt shaker,
the glass of water, the absence of light gathering
in the shadows of picture frames, they must be
naked and alone, they must stand for themselves.
My friend Henri and I arrived at this together in 1965
before I went away, before he began to kill himself,
and the two of us to betray our love. Can you taste
what I'm saying? It is onions or potatoes, a pinch
of simple salt, the wealth of melting butter, it is obvious,
it stays in the back of your throat like a truth
you never uttered because the time was always wrong,
it stays there for the rest of your life, unspoken,
made of that dirt we call earth, the metal we call salt,
in a form we have no words for, and you live on it.

Afterword

Sweat is leaven, bread, Ujamaa
Bread of the earth, by the earth
For the earth. Earth is all people.

This contemporary African farm poem has established roots. It's a hybrid voice spreading its root system from Australia's sprawling grasslands to its near-seedless outback. This vigorous voice takes hold year after year in poems from the grainfields of Mexico, India, and China. It's the sweat-thick voice of farmers, fieldworkers, hungry soldiers, fry-cooks and waiters, professors, shepherds, and midwives — all the earth's people.

The voice comes from any of the megacities, townships, or squatters' villages in the world. Weeks ago, in Sacramento, listening to Richard Rodriguez's brief telling of his earliest memories of California's Great Central Valley (which provides 50 percent of the nation's fresh fruit and vegetables), I was struck by his recounting of his mother's fear of the Central Valley's farm soil. During the questions and answers afterward, Rodriguez looks right at me when I ask: "After many years away from the fields of Mexico, does your mother still feel that same fear about the agricultural fields of the San Joaquin Valley?" "Yes," he answers (for all of us). "We are fated to the land." Stooping and sweaty with his own memory, Rodriguez becomes the voice of generations of Mexican, Vietnamese, Chinese, and Japanese laborers who stoop and squat to the Central Valley soil. During those moments when he recollects his family history — his mother's fear of the land — I too am squeezing a handful of soil into the shape of memory. I become Rodriguez. I am he, he is me: the soil of his labor, the laboring soil.

Now, driving through the Amana Colonies in Iowa, I'm visiting Iowa from California to complete the final draft of my second anthology of farm poems. (The first book, *Handspan of Red Earth: An Anthology of American Farm Poems*, is the best-selling poetry book ever from the University of Iowa Press.) I can look in any direction and list the agri-abundance: cornfields, soybean fields, cattle, and hogs. Nearing South Amana, I turn off at the junction of Highways

6 and 220, drive to the front steps of a century-old brick building, once the general store in South Amana. From the sign above the porch steps, above the store's tall double doors —FERN HILL— comes Dylan Thomas' memorable voice: "young and easy under the apple bough / About the lilting house and happy as the grass was green." As if the poet's memory opens the front doors of the store, Thomas' voice again: "Fields high as the house, the tunes from the chimney."

People love to farm their nostalgia for the soil. Where does the voice of the soil come from, I wonder as I fumble with a ceramic teacup and glance around at the star quilts, candies, honey jars, teddy bears, and braid rugs and inhale the spellbinding scent of chocolate-dipped orange rind.

"My husband wrote about the farm. He loved it," store owner Patti Walsh-Bailey tells me. "Could I see some of his farm poems?" I ask. S. A. Walsh's poems aren't what I expected: penciled drafts, typed drafts, edited and reedited, of many fragments on a single page. Every space on the page filled like fields planted all the way to the property line. Clearly, a man listening to the voice of the farm, who asks over each draft where the voice of the soil comes from. I tell Patti I'm reminded of my years of creative-writing classes at University of the Pacific in Stockton. Of drafts like these that find paper but not publishers. Of students who ponder the voice of the land around them. Students whom I've encouraged to bend to, squat to, and squeeze the soil and then write about its taste, its smell. I read Walsh's "R.F.D. Mailbox" a couple of times before I ask Patti for permission to include it in the forthcoming anthology.

"I have to tell you about him," Patti says, as she signs the permission form. "He had been ill. He was dying. I couldn't leave him alone. He was propped up on the sofa. The late-afternoon sun on his quilt, and then, the wind snagged the garbage can and flung it onto the porch. The wind slammed the can against the cement. The clanging. I wanted to go outside, but I couldn't leave him. He was almost breathless. I watched his breaths raise the green quilt, then almost no breath. The can hit the windowsill. I had to go out onto the porch. I nabbed the lid. Then, the wind rolled a three-foot-long cardboard tube up against my feet. There was a poster in the tube. I pulled the poster out of its sleeve and unrolled it to a gasping calico kitten's skinny body, strung out and dangling from the branch of a tree. At the bottom of the poster: HANG IN THERE. I took this voice in. I took the voice to be the Lord's. I went back into the parlor. I began writing in my journal. I worked as fast as I could. The green quilt at rest. His hands, his fingertips at rest on the stretches of green threading. When he moved, I went to his side. I thought he said, 'I am waiting for the Lord.' I bent to his cotton-green field. 'What, what?' I asked him. 'You are waiting for the Lord, is that it?' I put my ear to his mouth. He tried the watery air again, 'I'm . . .' 'What, what? Tell me,' I whispered." Patti looked out at the half-mile stretch of Iowa corn furrows, and she repeated Walsh's whisper, "'I am *writing* for the Lord,' he said."

What did Richard Rodriguez feel that Sunday evening in his home in Sacramento, when he slipped his fork into a Central Valley–grown tomato wedge or under a Salinas-harvested strawberry? Surely he felt something about his own organic fear of the soil. But perhaps he also heard himself say, this time with thanksgiving, about the soil of his family, "Fated to this blessed land."

Permissions

"Afraid of the Countryside" by Sakutaro Hagiwara from *Ten Japanese Poets*, Granite Publications, 1973.

"Agriculture" by James Galvin from *Lethal Frequencies*, 1995, reprinted by permission of Copper Canyon Press.

"And You, Vanya . . ." by Yury Odarchenko from *Twentieth Century Russian Poetry: Silver and Steel: An Anthology*, edited by Albert C. Todd and Max Hayward, with Daniel Weissbort, 1993, reprinted by permission of Bantam Doubleday Dell Publishing Group.

"Appetite" by Maxine Kumin from *The Long Approach*, 1985, reprinted by permission of Penguin Books, Curtis Brown, Ltd.

"At a Potato Digging" by Seamus Heaney from *Poems 1965–1975*, 1980, reprinted by permission of Farrar, Straus & Giroux and Faber and Faber Ltd.

"Aunt Julia" by Norman MacCaig from *Collected Poems*, 1985, reprinted by permission of the estate of the author and Chatto & Windus.

"Baobab Fruit Picking (or Development in Monkey Bay)" by Jack Mapanje from *The Chattering Wagtails of Mikuyu Prison*, 1989, reprinted by permission of Heinemann.

"The Barn-yard" by Sheila Cussons from *The Penguin Book of Southern African Verse*, 1989.

"Between Each Song" by A. R. Ammons from *American Poetry Review*, March/April 1997, Vol. 26, No. 2, reprinted by permission of the author.

"The Bitch" by Sergey Yesenin from *Twentieth Century Russian Poetry: Silver and Steel: An Anthology*, edited by Albert C. Todd and Max Hayward, with Daniel Weissbort, 1993, reprinted by permission of Bantam Doubleday Dell Publishing Group.

"The Biting Insects" by Galway Kinnell from *Imperfect Thirst*, 1994, reprinted by permission of Houghton Mifflin Co.

"The Bogie-Wife" by Kathleen Jamie from *Columbia: A Journal of Literature and Art*, 1996, reprinted by permission of *Columbia*, Graduate Writing Division of Columbia University School of the Arts.

"Bread and Wine" by Nina Cassian from *Life Sentence: Selected Poems*, 1990, reprinted by permission of W. W. Norton and Anvil Press Poetry, Ltd.

"The Broken Ground" by Wendell Berry from *Collected Poems*, 1985, reprinted by permission of North Point Press, a division of Farrar, Straus & Giroux.

"Buck" by Paul Zarzyski from *All This Way for the Short Ride: Roughstock Sonnets*, 1971–1996, reprinted by permission of the author and Museum of New Mexico Press.

"The Bull-Roarer" by Gerald Stern from *Bread Without Sugar*, 1992, reprinted by permission of W. W. Norton & Co.

"Cabbages at Night" by Hasegawa Ryusei from *Like Underground Water: The Poetry of Mid-Twentieth Century Japan*, translated by Naoshi Koriyama & Edward Lueders, 1995, reprinted by permission of Copper Canyon Press.

"Carbuncle" by Muriel Zeller, reprinted by permission of the author.

"Cattle" by Kijima Hajime from *Like Underground Water: The Poetry of Mid-Twentieth Century Japan*, translated by Naoshi Koriyama & Edward Lueders, 1995, reprinted by permission of Copper Canyon Press.

"Conversation at Midnight" by Adelina Adalis from *Twentieth Century Russian Poetry: Silver and Steel: An Anthology*, edited by Albert C. Todd and Max Hayward, with Daniel Weissbort, 1993, reprinted by permission of Bantam Doubleday Dell Publishing Group.

"The Cucumber" by Nazim Hikmet from *Poems of Nazim Hikmet*, translated by Randy Blasing and Mutlu Konuk, 1994, reprinted by permission of Persea Books.

"The Dead Calf" by Richard Jones from *At Last We Enter Paradise*, 1991, reprinted by permission of Copper Canyon Press.

"delta farm," by Dennis Schmitz from *String*, 1976, reprinted by permission of Ecco Press.

"De Profundis" by Georg Trakl from *Evidence of Fire: An Anthology of Twentieth Century German Poetry*, 1988, reprinted by permission of Owl Creek Press.

"Depths of Fields" by Luis Cabalquinto from *Returning a Borrowed Tongue*, edited by Nick Carbo, 1995, Coffee House Press, reprinted by permission of Nick Carbo.

"Downstream" by Linda Hussa, reprinted by permission of the author.

"The Earthworm" by Harry Edmund Martinson from *Friends, You Drank Some Darkness*, translated by Robert Bly, 1975, Faber & Faber Ltd., reprinted by permission of Robert Bly.

"Egg and Daughter Night, April 1951" by William Matthews from *Denver Quarterly*, reprinted by permission of the author.

"Everything Else You Can Get You Take" by Robert Dana from *Iowa Review*, 1986, Vol. 16, No. 2, reprinted by permission of the author.

"Faces at the First Farmworkers' Constitutional Convention" by José Montoya from *Information: Twenty Years of Joda*, 1992, Chusma House, reprinted by permission of the author.

"Farmer" by Jack Myers from *The Family War*, 1978, L'Epervier Press, reprinted by permission of the author.

"Farmers" by Kathleen Peirce from *Mercy*, 1991, reprinted by permission of University of Pittsburgh Press.

"Farm Labourer" by George Mackay Brown from *George Mackay Brown: Selected Poems, 1954–1992*, 1996, reprinted by permission of University of Iowa Press.

"Farm Wife" by Ellen Bryant Voigt from *Claiming Kin*, 1972, Wesleyan University Press. Reprinted by permission.

"Fat of the Land" by Georgiana Valoyce-Sanchez from *Home Places*, 1995, University of Arizona Press, reprinted by permission of the author.

"Flirting with a Pig" by Aleksandar Ristovic from *The Horse Has Six Legs: An Anthology of Serbian Poetry*, edited and translated by Charles Simic, 1992, reprinted by permission of Graywolf Press.

"Fruit" by Gabriela Mistral from *A Gabriela Mistral Reader*, translated by Maria Giachetti, edited by Marjorie Agosin, 1993, reprinted by permission of White Pine Press.

"The Funeral" by Norman Dubie from *The Springhouse*, 1986, reprinted by permission of W. W. Norton & Co.

"The Green Combine" by Janet Kauffman from *The Weather Book*, 1981, Texas Tech University Press. Reprinted by permission.

"Green Fields" by W. S. Merwin from *The Atlantic Monthly*, Vol. 275, No. 2, February 1995, reprinted by permission of the author.

"Heavier" by Pierre Reverdy from *Pierre Reverdy: Selected Poems*, translated by John Ashbery, 1991, Wake Forest Press. Reprinted by permission.

"The Hen" by Marvin Bell, reprinted by permission of the author.

"The Hill Farmer Speaks" by R. S. Thomas from *Speak To The Hills*, Aberdeen University Press, 1985. Reprinted by permission.

"Hoeing" by Gary Soto from *The Elements of San Joaquin*, 1977, University of Pittsburgh Press, reprinted by permission of the author.

"Horse-doctor" by Katherine Pierpoint from *Truffle Beds*, 1995, reprinted by permission of Faber and Faber Ltd.

"Hunger" by Kim Chi Ha from *Cry of the People and Other Poems*, 1974, Autumn Press, reprinted by permission of the author.

"In a Fallow Field in the North Is a Plow That Hurts Me" by Duo Duo from *Anthology of Modern Chinese Poetry*, edited and translated by Michelle Yeh, 1992, Yale University Press. Reprinted by permission.

"In Peru, the Quechans Have a Thousand Words for Potato" by Ray Gonzalez from *The Heat of Arrivals*, 1996, reprinted by permission of BOA Editions, Ltd.

"In the Pasture," by Jorie Graham from *The Errancy*, 1997, Ecco Press. Reprinted by permission.

"July 2nd, 1916" by Phoebe Hesketh from *The Leave Train: New and Selected Poems*, 1994, Enitharmon Press. Reprinted by permission.

"A Land of Drought" by Maxamed Cabdille Xasan from *An Anthology of Somali Poetry*, translated by B. W. Andrzejewski and Sheila Andrzejewski, 1993, reprinted by permission of Indiana University Press.

"Legacy" by Márton Kalász from *American Poetry Review*, 1981.

"A Leopard Lives in a Muu Tree" by Jonathan Kariara from *The Penguin Book of Modern African Poetry*, 1963.

"The Lithuanian Well" by Johannes Bobrowski from *Contemporary East European Poetry: An Anthology*, edited by Emery George, 1983, Oxford University Press.

"The Memory" by Maya Angelou from *And Still I Rise*, 1978, reprinted by permission of Random House, Inc. and reprint permission from *The Language They Speak Is Things to Eat*, 1994, Virago Press Ltd., Little, Brown and Co.

"Mississippi Mysteries, Continued" by Al Young from *Straight No Chaser*, Creative Arts Book Co. Reprinted by permission of the author.

"The Right Hand of the Mexican Farmworker in Somerset County, Maryland" by Martín Espada from *Trumpets from the Islands of Their Eviction*, 1987, reprinted by permission of Bilingual Press, Arizona State University.

"The Simple Truth" by Philip Levine, 1994, reprinted by permission of Alfred A. Knopf.

"Some Grass along a Ditch Bank" by Larry Levis from *Winter Stars*, 1985, reprinted by permission of University of Pittsburgh Press.

"Someone Else's Sugarcane" by João Cabral de Melo Neto from *Selected Poetry, 1937–1990*, 1994, Wesleyan University Press. Reprinted by permission.

"The Spring" by P. J. Kavanagh from *Collected Poems*, 1992, Carcanet Press. Reprinted by permission.

"Sprout" by Rumiko Kōra from *Other Side River*, 1995, translated by Leza Lowitz & Miyuki Aoyama, Stone Bridge Press. Reprinted by permission.

"Stomping the Beaver Palace" by Roger Weingarten from *Ghost Wrestling*, 1996, Godine, reprinted by permission of the author.

"Sugar Cane" by Faustin Charles from *The Expatriate*, 1969, London, reprinted by permission of the author.

"The Sugar Slave" by Thylias Moss from *Small Congregations*, 1983, Ecco Press, 1993. Reprinted by permission.

"Summer" by Binyo Ivanov, from *Clay and Star*, translated by Lisa Sapinkopf, 1992, Milkweed Press, reprinted by permission of the translator.

"Swineherd" by Eilean Ni Chuilleanain from *The Second Voyage*, 1977, Gallery Press and Wake Forest University Press. Reprinted by permission.

"They Plow" by Giovanni Pascoli from *Twentieth Century Italian Poetry*, translated by Marc Wolterbeek, University of Toronto Press. Reprinted by permission.

"Tractor" by Ted Hughes from *Moortown*, Faber and Faber Ltd. Reprinted by permission.

"The United Fruit Co." by Pablo Neruda from *Selected Poems of Pablo Neruda*, translated by Ben Belitt, 1961, Grove Press. Reprinted by permission.

"Untitled [*If you grab a chicken by its feet*]" by Tomaz Salamun from *The Selected Poems of Tomaz Salamun*, edited by Charles Simic, 1988, Ecco Press. Reprinted by permission.

"Washing the Grain" by Yasmine Gooneratne from *Australian Voices: Poetry and Prose of the 1970s*, 1975, Australian National University Press, reprinted by permission of the author.

"Waterpot" by Grace Nichols from *The Penguin Book of Caribbean Verse*, 1986.

"West Texas" by Langston Hughes from *Collected Poems*, 1994, reprinted by permission of Alfred A. Knopf.

"What If the World Stays Always Far Off " by Linda Gregg from *Too Bright To See*, 1981, reprinted by permission of Graywolf Press.